THE 1ST MICHIGAN COLORED REGIMENT

THE 1ST MICHIGAN COLORED REGIMENT

FREE MEN WHO FOUGHT SLAVERY

MAURICE IMHOFF

Published by The History Press
An imprint of Arcadia Publishing
Charleston, SC
www.historypress.com

First published 2025

Manufactured in the United States

ISBN 9781467158787

Library of Congress Control Number: 2025937582

Dedicated to grandparents such as mine, who instill in us a reverence for the past and a commitment to preserving our history. Their stories and guidance remind us that our heritage is a legacy worth safeguarding. May this book honor their dedication to illuminating the paths that shaped our journey.

Contents

Foreword, by Matt VanAcker 9
Preface 11

1. Setting the Scene 13
2. Emancipation Proclamation 17
3. Detroit Erupts 24
4. Detroit's Call for a Colored Regiment 26
5. Michigan's First Colored Regiment 28
6. Joining the Cause of Liberty 34
7. Camp Ward 47
8. A Grand Southern Tour 51
9. Barracks of Injustice: A Call for Dignity at Camp Ward 66
10. Presentation of the Colors 73
11. Strength in Unity 78
12. Returning for Justice: Colored Canadians Join the Fight 80
13. Trouble at Camp Ward 83
14. From Trouble to Triumph 92
15. The Refused Escort 95
16. Forward for Freedom's Cause 101
17. The 102nd United States Colored Troops 122

18. 1865: Marching Toward Liberation 138
19. Chipman's Fierce Right Wing 142
20. Clark's Left Wing 146
21. The Last Push for Freedom 149
22. Brothers in Arms to Neighbors in Peace 155
23. Preserving the Legacy of Freedom's Heroes 160

Epilogue 167
Notes 171
About the Author 187

Foreword

On January 5, 1864, a large crowd gathered at Camp Ward in Detroit, Michigan, to witness a special presentation ceremony. The Colored Ladies Soldiers Aid Society of Detroit of the city presented to the 1st Michigan Colored Infantry Regiment a beautiful battle flag. The regimental banner, with its field of blue emblazoned with the federal eagle, wings outstretched, bore the painted inscription, "All men are born free and equal, To realize which, we fight." It would be impossible to find a more fitting epitaph to the convictions of Michigan's community of color and the brave Black soldiers who would fight and die beneath those very colors, upholding the Union and finally ending the scourge of slavery in our nation.

At the time of this ceremony, the country was heading into the third year of the Civil War, "testing whether that nation or any nation so conceived and so dedicated can long endure." The war had ravaged the country, depleted its resources and left many graves and empty chairs across the peninsular state. In his 1863 annual message to the legislature, Michigan's wartime governor, Austin Blair, declared, "All the blood and carnage of this terrible war, all the heart-rending casualties of battle, and the sad bereavements occasioned by them, have the same cause—slavery. The greatest, vilest criminal of the world, it must perish." Perish it would, but only after the incalculable service and sacrifice of 90,000 Michigan soldiers, including 1,400 men of color, many of whom were born into slavery and had witnessed its brutality firsthand.

What were the conditions and underlying reasons that led so many Michiganders (well over half of the eligible male population) to leave their homes and hearth fires to fight in the Civil War? Some historians attribute this great contribution to the strength of the abolition cause in Michigan. Numerous routes and stations of the Underground Railroad were spread across the lower tier of Michigan counties, through which many members of the 1st Michigan Colored Regiment/102nd USCT had achieved their freedom. Jackson, Michigan, also held the distinction of being the birthplace of the Republican Party, the very party that would long be associated with slavery's demise. Other Michigan soldiers made it very clear, however, that they fought to uphold the Union and for no other higher purpose. As Michigan-born Colonel Charles A. Whittlesey wrote in 1862, "I fight to save the Union and the Constitution, not to free the negroes. I am no abolitionist."[1]

There can be very little question, however, regarding the motivation for the fight of Michigan's soldiers of color and the white men who officered their regiment, as declared in painted adornment on their flag. "All men are born free"—not just a chosen few who are born free based on the vagaries of some random birth lottery, but *all* men. "All men are born equal"—equal to make their own choices in life and death, equal to make the decision to fight to free others, to sacrifice one's own safety and security to make all men free, to quite literally "realize which we fight." The pride and courage these brave, Black men displayed on the battlefield, following their lovingly inscribed banner, may now receive its rightful due with the publication of *The 1st Michigan Colored Regiment: Free Men Who Fought Slavery*.

In his remarks to the regiment in Jackson, Michigan, Govern Blair proclaimed, "We have committed to your care the flag of our country. That you will fight for it no one doubts, and if per chance any of you shall fall, there will be a consolation that you will find honorable graves." Many of these Black soldiers did, in fact, find honor on the battlefield defending the flag of their country, a country that had most often treated them with disdain and disrespect, even while they shed their blood to preserve it. Many found their final resting places in those honorable graves, and their story will now be told.

—MATT VANACKER,
Author, *Lansing and the Civil War*, and
Michigan State Capitol Director of Education Emeritus/
Director of Save the Flags

Preface

Writing this book has been both a personal and collective journey—a tribute to the brave soldiers of the 102nd United States Colored Troops who fought for freedom, resilience and justice. As a descendant of enslaved individuals from Georgia, I feel a profound connection to these men who, despite having just escaped the bonds of slavery, chose to return to the South as soldiers. They came not merely as freedmen but as champions of liberty for those who remained in chains, bringing the weight of their own past and the hope of a brighter future. This book is a testament to their courage and sacrifice, a commitment to ensuring that their legacy remains alive and respected.

Leading the 102nd USCT Company C reenactors, a group of high school and college students, has deepened my understanding of the original regiment's many young soldiers. Those young men were just beginning their lives, yet they chose to risk everything for a cause greater than themselves. My thoughts often return to John Taylor, one of the regiment's brave young men who survived the war only to face a lynching in Michigan shortly after. His tragic story and the countless sacrifices of his comrades underscore the need for remembrance and justice. Through our living history events, my fellow students and I seek to honor them not only as historical figures but also as people whose struggles and resilience reverberate through history and still inspire us today.

To my family, especially my mother and my late grandfather, I owe a debt of gratitude for their unwavering support on this journey. My grandfather, in particular, was the one who introduced me to the study of history and the importance of preserving the past. His stories ignited my curiosity and instilled in me a responsibility to honor our ancestors' experiences. My mother has been my pillar, her encouragement a constant source of strength and motivation. This book would not have been possible without their love and guidance.

The Gospel Army Black History Group/102nd USCT Company C, to which I belong, has been invaluable in bringing this history to life through our living history demonstrations across Michigan. Educating diverse audiences and embodying figures like Private Parker Bon in events has been a privilege, providing me with firsthand experience in historical interpretation. Our reenactments, including those that recount battles like Honey Hill, remind us all of the 102nd's remarkable bravery and accomplishments on the battlefield—moments that brought honor to our ancestors and pride to our communities. I am grateful to my colleagues in this group who work tirelessly to ensure that these stories are not forgotten.

Finally, I extend my thanks to all who have supported this work, from friends to mentors to the young reenactors who join me in our mission. This book exists because of our shared commitment to history and remembrance. It is my hope that the stories of the 1st Michigan Colored Regiment/102nd United States Colored Troops inspire a renewed understanding of their fight for freedom, equality and respect—values we strive to uphold in their memory and in our ongoing journey.

Chapter I

Setting the Scene

African Americans in Michigan have a rich and resilient history that stretches back well before the Civil War. By the early nineteenth century, Michigan had already attracted Black settlers due to its proximity to Canada, where slavery was abolished in 1834. Michigan's location along the Underground Railroad made it a critical destination for formerly enslaved people seeking freedom, especially after the Fugitive Slave Act of 1850. Free Black communities formed in cities like Detroit, where residents helped organize resistance efforts against slave catchers and aided those seeking safety across the border. These early communities laid the groundwork for African Americans' involvement in Michigan's social and political life, driven by a collective mission to secure freedom and equal rights.[2]

In Detroit and other towns, African Americans built strong communal institutions, including churches and social organizations that offered support, education and advocacy. For example, Detroit's Second Baptist Church, founded in 1836, became a key Underground Railroad station and a center of activism for the Black community. The church's members, many of whom were former enslaved individuals, organized resources to help newly arrived Black residents, facilitating their transition to freedom. These early institutions allowed Michigan's Black community to cultivate a shared sense of identity and purpose while fostering leaders who would later advocate for broader civil rights.[3]

Throughout the 1840s and 1850s, Michigan's African American residents became more politically active, advocating for legal and social reform. Black

Michiganders participated in state and national conventions focused on abolition and civil rights, such as the 1858 convention in Detroit, where delegates from across the state gathered to discuss strategies for ending slavery. These conventions and gatherings amplified the voices of Michigan's Black residents and fostered collaborations between African American leaders and white abolitionists. Together, they worked to pressure local government officials and the broader public to resist slavery and support Black rights.[4]

Michigan's African American community also played a vital role in recruiting Black soldiers for the Union army. Even before the Emancipation Proclamation in 1863, Black residents of Michigan advocated for the right to fight for the Union cause. Detroit's Black leaders argued that African Americans, though denied many rights, should still have the opportunity to defend their freedom and prove their loyalty to the Union. This advocacy set the stage for Michigan's Black residents to enlist in units such as the 102nd U.S. Colored Troops, a regiment comprising Black soldiers who would go on to fight valiantly for the Union.[5]

By the onset of the Civil War, Michigan's African American community had established a legacy of resilience, activism and community-building. From forming networks along the Underground Railroad to establishing key institutions like Second Baptist Church and advocating for civil rights, Black Michiganders had created a strong foundation for themselves and future generations. Their efforts not only contributed to Michigan's social fabric but also advanced the broader struggle for freedom and equality in America.[6]

At the outbreak of the Civil War in 1861, African Americans faced both renewed opportunities and intense challenges. The war began on April 12, 1861, when Confederate forces attacked Fort Sumter, prompting a national crisis over slavery and unionism. While the war's early goals focused on preserving the Union, enslaved and free African Americans saw the conflict as a path to liberation. They immediately took steps to contribute to the Union cause, even though they were officially barred from joining the U.S. Army. Throughout 1861 and 1862, African Americans volunteered to serve in various capacities, from laborers and camp aides to guides and nurses, hoping to demonstrate their loyalty and contribute to the war effort.[7]

Even before the Emancipation Proclamation, free Black communities in Northern states like New York, Massachusetts and Pennsylvania advocated for the inclusion of Black soldiers. Black leaders like Frederick Douglass and Martin Delany argued that African Americans had both the right and duty to fight for their own freedom and the Union's survival. However, discriminatory policies and prevailing racist attitudes prevented them from enlisting as combat soldiers. In some cases, African Americans who tried to enlist were turned away or relegated to labor-intensive support roles rather than receiving arms and training. This exclusion highlighted the contradictions of a war waged by the Union to secure freedom without offering that freedom to African Americans.[8]

Despite these restrictions, enslaved people in the South began taking bold steps to escape and support the Union cause as soon as the war began. Early in the war, enslaved individuals sought refuge in Union-occupied territories, forcing Union generals to address the issue of escaped slaves, or "contrabands." In May 1861, General Benjamin Butler declared that enslaved individuals who escaped to Union lines would be considered "contraband of war" and therefore not returned to their enslavers. This policy allowed the Union to harbor and employ thousands of African Americans as laborers, aiding the Union war effort while offering some freedom, although they still remained officially barred from combat.[9]

As the war progressed, African Americans played crucial roles in intelligence gathering and reconnaissance for Union forces. Due to their familiarity with Southern terrain and local customs, many enslaved individuals who escaped to Union lines provided valuable information on Confederate troop movements and supply routes. This intelligence proved essential for Union victories in numerous battles. African American women, too, contributed to the war effort by acting as cooks, laundresses and nurses, serving soldiers and refugees in Union camps and hospitals. Although these contributions were not recognized as formal military service, they underscored African Americans' commitment to the Union cause and their own liberation.[10]

By 1862, mounting pressure from abolitionists and African American leaders, combined with military setbacks, led the Union government to reconsider its stance on Black enlistment. Many military officials, including Secretary of War Edwin Stanton, recognized that incorporating African Americans into the Union army would bolster manpower and weaken the Confederacy, which relied heavily on enslaved labor to support its own war effort. These debates set the stage for the Emancipation Proclamation, issued in September 1862 and taking effect on January 1, 1863. Although it initially freed enslaved individuals only in Confederate states, the proclamation also authorized the enlistment of Black soldiers, marking a major shift in the Union's military policy.[11]

African Americans' involvement in the Civil War prior to the Emancipation Proclamation illustrates their determination to seize freedom and rights despite official obstacles. They contributed in every way available to them, from laboring in support roles to gathering intelligence and advocating for their own inclusion in the Union army. This dedication laid the groundwork for the eventual formation of regiments like the U.S. Colored Troops, which would go on to make significant contributions to Union victories and ultimately the abolition of slavery. The actions of African Americans before 1863 helped shape the Union war effort and demonstrated the importance of their role in America's fight for freedom.[12]

Chapter 2

Emancipation Proclamation

The Emancipation Proclamation, issued by President Abraham Lincoln on January 1, 1863, was a landmark document in the American Civil War. Although it did not immediately free all enslaved individuals, it declared the freedom of slaves in the Confederate states in rebellion against the Union. The Proclamation strategically shifted the war from a battle solely about preserving the Union to a fight for human freedom, allowing Lincoln to enlist former enslaved individuals as soldiers to further weaken the Confederacy. The Proclamation also marked the first legal acceptance of African American soldiers in the Union army, as they were now recognized as potential contributors to the Union war effort.[13]

Prior to the Civil War, Black men had fought in earlier American conflicts, including the Revolutionary War and the War of 1812, often in volunteer capacities without official recognition or equal status. These early instances showcased Black men's willingness to serve, but it was not legally sanctioned for them to enlist in the regular U.S. Army. The Militia Act of 1792 explicitly restricted militia service to white men, reflecting racial prejudice and the systemic exclusion of Black people from official military roles. Despite this, African Americans saw each conflict as an opportunity to challenge the status quo and fight for their own freedom and rights, even if it meant unofficial or unacknowledged participation.[14]

The Emancipation Proclamation, however, changed that framework by legally allowing Black men to enlist in the Union army. Lincoln's administration recognized that Black soldiers would strengthen the Union

A Union soldier in uniform stands holding an upraised sword in his right hand and an American flag in his left, with a banner reading "Freedom to the slave." In the back left, African Americans enter the door of a "Public School." At right, another soldier removes manacles from the wrists of a shirtless, kneeling African American, while a formation of colored troops marches off in the back right. *University of Michigan.*

forces numerically and symbolically, rallying support for the cause of abolition both domestically and internationally. The Proclamation thus opened the doors for more than 180,000 African American men to serve in the U.S. Colored Troops (USCT), established shortly thereafter. Their contributions became invaluable, with Black soldiers fighting in crucial battles such as the Siege of Port Hudson and the Battle of Fort Wagner, helping to tip the scales toward Union victory.[15]

While the Proclamation legalized Black enlistment, African American soldiers still faced significant discrimination. They were initially paid less than white soldiers and assigned to separate units, with fewer opportunities for promotion. Nevertheless, their courage and dedication challenged prevailing racial biases and demonstrated the capabilities and commitment of African Americans in the fight for the Union and freedom. Their service helped change public opinion on Black soldiers, paving the way for a more integrated military in future conflicts.[16]

The Emancipation Proclamation was thus a turning point for both the Union army and African Americans, laying a legal foundation that allowed Black soldiers to fight openly and officially for the first time in American history. This participation strengthened the Union army, undermined Confederate efforts and marked a significant step toward the eventual goal of equality. The bravery of African American soldiers during the Civil War left an enduring legacy, inspiring future generations and advancing the struggle for civil rights in the United States.[17]

On that historic day for the nation, January 1, 1863, Detroit's Black community gathered to offer gratitude to both God and President Lincoln. At the Lafayette Street African Methodist Episcopal Church, the powerful sense of liberation was palpable. John Molane, J. Bird and G. Hodges were promptly commissioned to draft joyful resolutions pertaining to the news. As this committee moved to craft the documents, the congregation joined in singing "Blow Ye the Trumpet, Blow" and listened eagerly to the bearers of good news. The committee returned from their meeting bringing forth the following resolution:

> *RESOLVED, That we thank God for putting it into the heart of Abraham Lincoln, to proclaim liberty to the colored race; because it works benefit not only to four millions of colored men but to five millions of white men, called in the South "poor white trash" who have no education, and their masters, the slave-owners, are determined they shall have none, and they are, therefore, fit only for filibustering, and carrying out the cursed designs of the*

slavery propagandists at the South, and their vile supporters at the North. We believe that slavery makes labor disrespectable, and any country in this state, must necessarily remain under the curse of God, until such evils are removed. We hail the emancipation as a great good to mankind. We hail it with joyful acclamation, and shall only await for the morrow to see more plainly and perfectly developed the idea and principles of the President. May God bless Abraham Lincoln and the people.[18]

On January 6, 1863, just days after the Emancipation Proclamation was issued, a significant and more widely known gathering took place at the Second Baptist Church in Detroit. The city's African American community convened at the church to celebrate President Lincoln's historic act, which freed more than 3 million enslaved individuals. The church was filled to capacity with people of African descent—young and old, wealthy and poor alike.

During the meeting, a letter was read that conveyed the sentiments of some white citizens, sharing in the joy of the moment:

Detroit, Jan. 6, 1863

To John D. Richards, William Webb, and William Lambert:
It is proposed to have 50,000 copies of the President's Emancipation Proclamations of September 22d and January 1st, printed and sent by Express to the Michigan regiments now in the field. The cost will be $350, and while $250 will be raised by the white people of our town to defray this expense it is thought that the colored people will cheerfully contribute the remainder for the purpose of sending this Great Bill of Rights to their friends in the Southern States at their homes who are to be benefitted thereby.—C.A. Trowbridge[19]

After several speakers addressed the assembly, several preambles and resolutions were unanimously passed by those present:

Whereas, The Institution of Slavery has existed in this country from the foundation to the present hour, brutalizing its victims, and at times depriving them of every means of elevation, closing upon them every avenue to knowledge, and shrouding their minds in the gloom of artificial night; and

Second Baptist Church, where it moved in 1857, after its founding in 1836. Established by thirteen formerly enslaved individuals, the church was a response to racial discrimination at the First Baptist Church and became a center for worship, abolitionist activities and civil rights advocacy. This location also served as a key station on the Underground Railroad, providing critical support to freedom-seekers before they crossed the Canadian border. In September 1865, Second Baptist Church hosted the Second Colored Men's State Convention, where delegates, despite internal conflict over representation that led to the creation of the Equal Rights League of Michigan, aligned with the National Equal Rights League to advocate for African American citizenship and voting rights for men. *Detroit Public Library Burton Historical Collection.*

WHEREAS, In the progressive march of events this monstrous iniquity has in the Province of God been swept from the land—the chains loosened from the heads of the captives—the prison doors opened and the oppressed set free—the year of jubilee proclaimed throughout the land, And, whereas, our hearts have been made to rejoice, by this triumph of truth over error—this accomplishment of the object for which in the silent watches of the night we have poured out our souls to Him who controls the destinies of nations—this achievement for which the blood of Lovejoy was shed, and for which a band of martyrs, countless in number, but bold in the sacred cause of truth, have been sacrificed on the altar of Liberty; and

WHEREAS, We recognize in this dispensation of Divine Providence an evidence of that irrepressible conflict between opposing and enduring forces; which must at last culminate in the establishment of universal right and the overthrow of universal wrong; therefore be it

RESOLVED, That when, in the course of human events, there comes a day which is destined to be an everlasting beacon light, marking a joyful era in the progress of a nation and the hopes of a people, it seems to be fitting the occasion that it should not pass unnoticed by those whose hopes it comes to brighten and to bless.

RESOLVED, That we render, first to God and then to Abraham Lincoln, our most profound and heartfelt thanks for the great triumph of Liberty over Slavery, in which four millions of our oppressed brethren have been raised from the depths of slavery to the level of free American citizens.

RESOLVED, That the name of Abraham Lincoln shall be treasured by us in holy remembrance as a man, who, despite the opposition of the Border States, or the weak-kneed of his northern friends, had the courage to declare, that freedom for all men was hereafter to be the policy of the government; that we will teach our children to thank him for this great act of Emancipation and seek to send his name down the pathway of the future, with that of Moses, as the deliverer from bondage of an oppressed people.

RESOLVED, That in this hour of the Nations peril, we are ready when called up on to buckle on our armor in defence of the Liberty which has been given to our Southern Brethren, and if in the fort or the field, on shipboard or meeting the enemies of constitutional right in the deadly conflict, we will prove that we are not traitors, but willing to defend the land of our birth.

> *RESOLVED, That although Judge Taney in the Dred Scott case sought to establish the idea, that we bad no rights which white men were bound to respect; we are glad to know that Edward Bates, the able Attorney General of the U.S., in a clear and forcible letter to the Sec'y of the Treasury, has scattered the sophistries of the prejudiced Judge, like chaffs before the wind, and established the fact beyond the power of refutation, that birth on the soil always secures the right of citizenship.*[20]

As expected, *Detroit Free Press* was critical of the Emancipation Proclamation, directing its commentary at Detroit's Black community with a mix of mockery and argument. The publication leaned heavily on constitutional grounds, asserting that President Lincoln lacked the authority to abolish slavery. Nonetheless, its primary means of attack were scornful remarks. In an article titled "The Ethiopians on the Proclamation," the *Detroit Free Press* wrote, "The colored portion of our free American population are highly jubilant over the Presidential Proclamation and are expressing their joy in various and sundry ways such as only these brutish beings can invent. 'Fader Abe,' as he is affectionately known by his colored brethren, has given them their Fourth of July."[21]

In contrast, another local newspaper acknowledged that while the Emancipation Proclamation was not a perfect solution, it represented progress: "The text of the Proclamation shows that it was issued purely as a war measure. There is no pretense of philanthropy, although in this regard the most magnificent results will flow from it."[22]

Chapter 3

Detroit Erupts

In March 1863, Detroit erupted into a race riot that is often misunderstood or incompletely reported. While the aftermath of the chaos is documented, the events leading up to it are frequently overlooked. Many assume that the Detroit Riot mirrored the Draft Riots in New York, and while there are parallels, the roots of Detroit's violence were more specific. The Union Draft Law, passed that month, angered many Northern working-class citizens who saw the war as a campaign to free enslaved people who would then compete for jobs. The draft law's preference for the wealthy only deepened the resentment. Heightened tensions were further fueled by inflammatory speeches and reckless reporting.[23]

The key trigger for the Detroit Riot of 1863 was the Faulkner case. William Faulkner, a forty-two-year-old Black man who ran a restaurant, was accused of molesting two nine-year-old girls: Mary Brown, who was white, and Ellen Hoover, who was African American. This case drew intense public interest, and local newspapers amplified the drama by referring to Faulkner as "the Negro Faulkner." As Faulkner was being escorted from the courthouse back to jail, a crowd gathered, aiming to seize him. The sheriff, anticipating trouble, had requested military assistance. Tensions escalated rapidly, and when a soldier opened fire, killing a bystander named Charles Langer, the scene descended into violence.[24]

The crowd transformed into a frenzied mob, launching an assault on the colored community with unrestrained aggression. What had begun as an angry crowd became a force of destruction, indiscriminately attacking anyone of Black, brown or mixed heritage. An eyewitness, a colored resident of Detroit, recounted the terror and confusion, describing how he saw the mob, initially chasing individuals, grow larger as they swarmed the streets on foot and in wagons laden with beer. The mob, fueled by chaos and alcohol, became more violent as it reached the jail.[25]

The eyewitness described how shots rang out, sending people fleeing in panic. He observed members of the crowd brandishing weapons and threatening to kill any Black person they found. The mob's energy was directed at destroying homes and businesses, shattering windows and breaking down doors. The witness himself narrowly escaped harm, defending his house with a gun alongside a friend armed with an axe. Four times, the mob approached his door but retreated when he raised his weapon. From an upstairs window, he later watched as the mob demolished the cooper shop of Whitney Reynolds, the largest Black-owned cooper shop in the city.[26]

To quell the violence, authorities called in reinforcements from Detroit's Fort Wayne, and the 27th Michigan Infantry was dispatched from Ypsilanti. It took significant effort to restore order. By the end of the riot, between thirty and thirty-five homes belonging to colored families had been destroyed, more than two hundred Black residents were left homeless and two colored individuals had been killed, with many others injured. In a tragic turn, it was later revealed that Mary Brown had lied. Seven years after the event, she admitted to fabricating her accusation. Faulkner, who had been imprisoned at Jackson Prison, was released, but his health had deteriorated due to the ordeal; he died shortly after his release. His friends had supported him in starting a new business, but the damage had already been done.[27]

In the aftermath, the *Detroit Advertiser & Tribune* criticized the *Detroit Free Press* for its racially charged rhetoric and hypocrisy. In an effort to counteract the negative portrayals and highlight the Black community's role in the war, the publication ran stories showcasing their contributions. One such account focused on William H. Tiflin, who had served as a servant to Captain Graves of the 1st Michigan Infantry (white). During the Battle of Bull Run, Tiflin stepped up when the regiment's color sergeant was killed, heroically carrying the flag until he, too, was wounded in the heat of battle.[28]

Chapter 4

Detroit's Call for a Colored Regiment

As the year progressed, the *Detroit Advertiser & Tribune* expressed its dismay over the fact that many promising Black men were traveling to Massachusetts to join its renowned Black regiment. The publication questioned, "Why can't we form a Negro regiment in our own state, sparing these men a long journey and helping reduce our draft quota in the process?" During this period, Charles Lenox Remond, a prominent Black abolitionist, delivered an address at the Colored Baptist Church on Croghan Street in Detroit titled "The Lesson of the Hour to Colored Men." Although the speech's full text was not printed, it likely aimed to inspire his fellow men with a call to patriotic duty.[29]

Gradually, the narrative shifted, and Black men came to be seen as essential participants in the war effort. An editorial titled "The Colored Men and Their Claims" urged Black individuals from both the North and South to join the fight for freedom, suggesting that a strong regiment could be formed from the region. The piece concluded with a plea: "Give the colored men of Michigan the chance they have been so long wishing for." Just days later, the paper reported that a group of men from Battle Creek had enlisted in the 54th Massachusetts Regiment, noting that it was unjust for Michigan's men to bolster another state's ranks and quotas, ultimately increasing the likelihood of local men being drafted. In the same issue, a recruiting officer from Massachusetts, stationed in Detroit, revealed that more than two hundred colored men had enlisted there for the 54th.[30]

The newspapers publicly cast their doubt on the motives of the ruling party, questioning why President Lincoln was reluctant to authorize a Black regiment from Michigan. Critics argued that the proposal for such a regiment was a farce and labeled it a political ploy. They claimed that Michigan's Democratic Party supported the idea of sending every colored man out of the state to fight, even suggesting that if enough colored soldiers could not be found, the gap should be filled with abolitionists, regardless of age. This struggle to meet enlistment quotas was a widespread issue. One historian noted that frustrations in the capital often targeted recruiting agents and brokers who, despite watchful provost marshals at the train stations, managed to recruit colored men to meet Northern quotas, lured by substantial bounties. While some in Washington opposed integrating schools or sharing public spaces with colored citizens, they welcomed them as soldiers with open arms. As the conversation grew increasingly larger, Detroit would see numerous rallies—which likely included songs, passionate speeches and poetry—aimed at encouraging colored men to enlist in the Massachusetts colored regiments.[31]

Chapter 5

Michigan's First Colored Regiment

The editor of the *Detroit Advertiser & Tribune*, Henry Barns, was determined to get authorization to raise a colored regiment for the State of Michigan. This, however, was a difficult task. In 1862, the Michigan legislature had revised the Militia Act so only white men were eligible to enlist in Michigan regiments. Barns was a well-known Detroiter. He began his career in journalism in 1837 as a writer for the *Detroit Free Press* and remained on the editorial staff for fourteen years. Along with several other individuals, Barns established the *Detroit Tribune* in 1851. This newspaper later merged with the *Detroit Advertiser*, and Barns became the editor of the *Detroit Advertiser & Tribune*.[32]

During the spring of 1863, Barns approached Michigan's governor, Austin Blair, for permission to organize a Black regiment. Blair was in favor of raising Black troops and had previously applied to the federal government for permission to recruit Black soldiers, but he could not organize a colored regiment without consent from Washington. For this reason, Blair denied Barns's request to raise a colored regiment.[33]

After this request was denied, Barns appealed directly to Secretary of War Edwin M. Stanton. A few months later, Governor Blair received orders from the secretary of war to raise a colored regiment in Michigan. With this order, Stanton suggested that it "would be gratifying if you should give such authority to Mr. Barns":[34]

War Department
Washington, July 24th, 1863.

GOVERNOR, H. Barns, Esq., of Detroit, has applied to this department for authority to raise a regiment of colored troops in your State. The department is very anxious that such regiments should be raised, and authorizes you to raise them by volunteering under regulations of the department, a copy of which is submitted to you by the chief of the bureau, and it would be gratifying if you would give such authority to Mr. Barnes [sic]. *It seems to me that there has been some misunderstanding upon this subject, and I am informed that you were under the impression that the department would not authorize it. Until suitable arrangements could be made for the organization of the bureau, it was not deemed advisable to raise such troops, but the organization of colored troops is now a distinct bureau in the department, and is fully recognized as any other branch of the military service, and every encouragement is given by the department to the raising of such troops.*

Yours truly,
EDMIN M. STANTON
Secretary of War.[35]

—

His excellency, AUSTIN BLAIR,
Governor of Michigan, Jackson

His Excellency, Austin Blair, Governor of Michigan, Jackson, Mich.

SIR, I am instructed by Secretary of War to inform you that you are hereby authorized to raise one regiment of infantry to be composed of colored men, to be mustered into the United States service for three years, or during the war.

To these troops no bounties will be paid. They will receive ten dollars per month and one ration per day, three dollars of which monthly pay will be in clothing.

The organization of the regiment of the regiment must conform in all respects with the requirements of General Orders No. 110, War Department 1863, a copy of which is herewith enclosed.

The prescribed number of commissioned officers will be appointed in accordance with the provisions of General Orders Nos. 143 and 114,

War Department, current serious, of which please find enclosed. The officers thus appointed will be mustered into service on the presentation to the mustering officers of their appointments, signed by the Secretary of War. The appointments will be made to keep pace with the muster into server of the several companies. Thus, on information being received from you that the first company has been mustered into service, the necessary appointments for the company will be made. When four companies have been mustered in the lieutenant colonel of the regiment will be appointed, and so on in the accordance with the "Revised Mustering Regulations."

WAR DEPARTMENT
ADJUTANT GENERAL'S OFFICE
Washington. D.C. July 25th, 1863.[36]

On August 12, 1863, Michigan Adjutant General John Robertson informed Barns that he was authorized to raise a colored regiment:

Sir—The Governor of this State has been requested by the Secretary of War, in a letter under date of 24th ultimo, to give you authority to raise a regiment of colored troops in this State. I am instructed by the Governor to inform you that you are fully authorized and empowered to raise and organize such a regiment, under the instructions from the War Department, which are herewith enclosed, and under such restrictions as the Governor may deem proper to enjoin you.[37]

Military Department, Michigan
Adjutant General's Office
Detroit, August 12, 1863.

A separate letter from C.W. Foster, assistant adjutant general for the War Department, written to Austin Blair outlined some of the restrictions for this new regiment:

Sir—I am instructed by the Secretary of War to inform you that you are hereby authorized to raise one regiment of infantry to be composed of colored men, to be mustered into the United State service for three years, or during the war. To these troops no bounties will be paid. They will receive ten dollars per month and one ration per day, three dollars of which may be in clothing.[38]

Left: Henry Barns (April 1815–1871) was an influential figure in Detroit's journalism and politics scenes, born in Appledore Heath, Ashford Borough, Kent, England. He learned the printer's trade before immigrating to the United States, where he published a newspaper in Niles, Michigan, and became associated with the *Detroit Free Press*, notably supplying a printing press after a fire destroyed its facilities in 1837. In 1849, Barns was a founding member, chief editor and proprietor of the *Detroit Tribune*, dedicating several years to the paper in various roles. He served as postmaster of Detroit in 1866 and as a government pension agent from 1867 to 1869, as well as clerk of the House of Representatives in 1855. A staunch advocate for African American troops during the Civil War, he successfully recruited the first regiment of colored troops in 1863. Tragically, Barns was found dead in 1871, presumed to have died by suicide due to financial difficulties, leaving behind a legacy marked by his contributions to journalism and military service. *Michigan State Capitol.*

Right: Edwin McMasters Stanton (1814–1869) was the U.S. secretary of war during most of the Civil War, known for his firm leadership in organizing the Union war effort and overseeing the military strategy that led to the North's victory. *Library of Congress.*

The letter also outlined a timetable for the appointment of officers and a timetable for when the appointments were to be made. Noteworthy in this letter were the terms of pay, which were much lower than that of white regiments. A private in other infantry regiments was typically paid thirteen dollars a day and was provided clothing. Additionally, by this point in time men enlisting were eligible for substantial bounties to encourage enlistment.

One other regulation for the regiment required all officers of the regiment to be white. Colored soldiers were able to be noncommissioned officers, and the highest rank they were able to attain was sergeant major.[39]

The Democratic-leaning *Detroit Free Press* newspaper denounced the recruitment of colored troops as a deceptive ploy, calling it "a game of plunder for patronage, commissions, and contracts." It accused both the editor of the *Detroit Advertiser & Tribune*, Henry Barns, and the colored men he supported of being unwilling to leave the state for actual combat. In a particularly inflammatory remark, the editorial declared it fitting that Barns led the regiment, since his paper had "educated negroes to hate white men," and claimed that "negroes…ought to have been consulted in the selection, and not have an obnoxious white man forced upon them as a 'nigger-head' or leader." Beyond attacking Barns personally, the paper sought to discredit the legitimacy and sincerity of the Black regiment itself. It argued that neither Barns nor "the negro man under him" could be induced to fight, claiming that real service had already been rendered by those who joined white regiments long ago. The paper portrayed the new regiment as a political stunt, accusing the Republican Party of arming colored men merely to suppress white Democratic conscripts during the draft and elections.[40]

In response, a Republican-aligned journal sharply criticized this stance, defending the formation of Michigan's "Sable Arms" regiment and noting the return of John S. Bagg to the editorial team of the *Detroit Free Press*. The piece stated, "John S. Bagg has recently rejoined the editorial staff of the *Detroit Free Press* and now holds significant control over its content. This association fits seamlessly, amplifying the paper's pro-'amalgamation,' anti-Black, and divisive Copperhead tendencies." In an unexpected move three days later, the *Detroit Free Press* published an editorial that, despite its general disdain for the concept of a "black regiment," admitted that it preferred forming such a unit over the prospect of a draft.[41]

The newly approved Michigan volunteer regiment was raised to be raised as the 1st Michigan Colored Infantry Regiment. Recruiting began on August 12, 1863. The appointed officers came from multiple states, including Ohio, Illinois, New York, Georgia and South Carolina. Michigan communities were also represented in the officer ranks, as there were officers from Marshall, Grand Rapids, Alpena, Bath, Ann Arbor, Ypsilanti and Detroit. The appointment of these officers did not come immediately. The regulations of the War Department in Washington, D.C., pertaining to the enlistment of colored troops did not permit the appointment of officers beforehand. Applications for commissions in the colored regiments had to be accompanied with good vouchers as to the habits, moral character, military experience and general fitness to command. They were also required to have the endorsement or recommendation of the officers of their current or former regiment in which they had served. The original call for applicants noted that they must be Michigan men to receive attention. However, as described, several officers came from out of state. All appointments for the white officers had to go through the Board of Inspection in Washington, D.C., or Cincinnati, Ohio.[42]

Chapter 6

Joining the Cause of Liberty

In an article from the *Cass Country Republican* newspaper, Colonel Henry Barns said the following to the area's Black population:

> *The prompt active co-operation of colored men, and all friends of the measure, and every part of Michigan, it is earnestly so lieited* [sic] *to exert their influence to procure recruits to fill up the first Michigan regiment as speedily as possible. Colored men are authorized to procure men, and an enlistment fee of Two Dollars will be paid by the Government for all accepted men as soon as mustered and period-colored men of good character and capacity will secure noncommissioned positions in companies according to influence exerted and number of men secured.*[43]

Before it was legal in the United States to enlist Black soldiers to fight in the Union army, you could find Black men or young boys serving in labor roles as "contrabands" or "servants." This was the case for a twenty-seven-year-old Black gentleman of Detroit named Mr. Parker Bon. He was born in Cincinnati, Ohio, in 1837 and moved to Detroit in 1856. Bon was an employed servant at Detroit's Fort Wayne, often cooking in the officers' mess hall. During his time there, he spent many hours studying the military tactics through personal observation. He also spent time reading from the best authors on military maneuvers of the period. When the 1st Michigan Colored Regiment was being raised, there was a need for an efficient person of color to orchestrate the new troops. The officers of the regiment made

A Bit of War History: The Contraband, by Thomas Waterman Wood. *Metropolitan Museum of Art.*

some inquiries among Detroit's Black population to find someone to serve in this role. Mr. George De Baptiste created a petition, which was then signed by Messrs. Lambert, Cullen, Hodge and other prominent Black community members encouraging Colonel Barns to appoint Mr. Parker Bon as drill master for the regiment.[44]

Following this effort, Bon was sent to be examined by a board, which deemed him to be sufficient and encouraged to enlist in the Michigan's newly forming regiment. On September 16, 1863, Bon enlisted in the regiment, immediately being promoted to the rank of sergeant major, the highest rank a Black soldier could reach during the period. The cook who originally couldn't take part in the action was now instructing troops of his own community on how to be a Union soldier. Bon served throughout the war and was honorably discharged at the end of the conflict, receiving several recognitions as a noncommissioned officer and soldier. After the war, Mr. Parker Bon went back to civilian life, becoming an old paper dealer, which brought in a good amount of money. He lived to be fifty-six.[45]

A good number of enlistees had been mustered into the regiment wearing the uniform of the Union by September 25, 1863. The first company was expected to be filled within the next week. The men were given the blue suit just as fast as they mustered into service with the regiment. The *Advertiser & Tribune* reported that "already our citizens are becoming familiar with the sight of sturdy negroes, in bright accoutrements, passing along our avenues with proud steps and heads erect, apparently proud of their reception into the service of Uncle Sam—into the army fighting for the restoration of the Union and the freedom of their race." Henry Barns worked hard throughout this time of service to show that colored men could make good soldiers. One of the ways he showed off the men was by securing them quality uniforms. The uniforms given to the soldiers of the colored regiment were some of the best available. To enhance their appeared, the early soldiers of the regiment were recruited with brass shoulder scales.[46]

Kinchen Artis (1831–1905) was born in Logan County, Ohio, and enlisted at the age of thirty-seven. *Archives of Michigan.*

An article published on September 18, 1864, in the *Detroit Advertiser & Tribune* offered a stern rebuke of the *Detroit Free Press* for its attempts to undermine the formation of a colored regiment in Michigan. The paper was firm in its defense of the regiment, accusing the *Detroit Free Press*, the most powerful Democratic newspaper, of exhibiting a "chronic hatred of Michigan Colored men" and of seizing every opportunity to "belie and vilify them," along with anyone who sought to uplift them. The *Tribune* went on to specifically call out the *Detroit Free Press* for its hypocritical stance: while claiming to support the enlistment of Black Michiganders in regiments from other states, the *Free Press* actively opposed enlistment into a local Michigan-raised regiment. This contradiction, the paper argued, revealed the paper's true motives, not concern for military strategy or efficiency but rather a desire to discourage Michigan's colored residents from enlisting and aiming to deny them of the dignity and recognition of serving under their own state's banner.[47]

The *Detroit Advertiser & Tribune* was appalled by the *Free Press*'s insistence that it "makes any difference who enlists the colored men who desire to enter the army." This sentiment was rejected outright. The article asserted that there was, in fact, a "wide difference." Michigan needed to fill its own quotas, and every man, white or colored, enlisted in another state's regiment was one less counted toward Michigan's total. To drain Michigan of its colored volunteers was to sabotage the state's efforts and force it closer to an unpopular draft.[48]

In the final portion of the article, the *Detroit Advertiser & Tribune* turned its attention to a particularly inflammatory accusation by the *Free Press*, which had questioned the legitimacy of those involved in recruiting for the 1st Michigan Colored Regiment. The *Detroit Free Press* mockingly demanded a list of officers, "his Lieutenants, his Captains, his Majors, and Lieutenant Colonels," casting doubt on whether the regiment's organizers had any authority at all. In response, the *Tribune* condemned the statement as either "inexcusably ignorant or willfully malicious," making clear that no commission could be issued without a formal examination by a military board and approval from the adjutant general in Washington. The article explained that applicants needed to travel to Washington or Cincinnati for evaluation, a process slowed by the fact that many qualified candidates were still serving in the field.[49]

Despite the negative campaign by the Democratic-leaning paper, the *Tribune* confidently affirmed that the 1st Michigan Colored Regiment was moving forward. The paper emphasized that its organizers intended to staff the unit with experienced Michigan soldiers and had already submitted names for officer consideration weeks earlier. While acknowledging the bureaucratic delays, it dismissed the *Free Press*'s rhetoric as petty and irrelevant, stating bluntly, "We care nothing" for its doubts or attempts at ridicule. In a final declaration of resolve, the editorial concluded that "good officers will appear in good time" and that they did not regret the *Free Press*'s opposition—only that such opposition revealed the paper's hostility to Black enlistment and Michigan's own contribution to the Union war effort.[50]

On September 29, 1863, several well-known men of Detroit's colored community addressed the colored men of Michigan in the *Detroit Advertiser & Tribune*. They wrote the following in hopes to inspire men of African descent to join the newly formed regiment:

> *Gentlemen:—In 1620 two ships arrived in the United States filled with emigrants. One landed at Plymouth Rock, in Massachusetts, are bore a people fleeing from oppression, who commenced the settlement of this land upon the idea that all men ought to be free; and the other landed at Jamestown, in Virginia, filled with slaves, whose pretended owners sought to establish a great slaveholding oligarchy, which should rule the land forever. They sought to establish two separate and distinct civilizations—one a civilization of Liberty and Christianity, the other a civilization of Slavery and oppression. Both launched their barks upon the ocean of existence, and appealed to the sentiment of mankind for approval and protection. The ideas, the thoughts, the actions of the original settlers of the two sections, in due time took possession of those who followed, until the United States presented to the world the strange paradox of a land of liberty filled with slaves.*
>
> *But it was impossible for such a state of affairs to exist for ever. It was written as unmistakably as the decrees of Fate, that Freedom and Slavery could not live together in the same land. The men who made the Constitution of the country hoped they could conciliate the people and make the matter palatable and agreeable to both sections; and although they had a land filled with slavery, they made no positive or stringent provisions for its protection in that instrument. They were willing to permit freedom and slavery, if possible, to live together under the same flag; but as well expect fire and powder to keep quit in the same cannon. An explosion must come; and in April, 1861 when the first cannon belched its venom on Fort Sumter, it sounded the death-knell of American Slavery, while at the same time it called to arms the Slavemongers of the South for its protection and defense. They submitted their cause to arbitrament of the sword, and have marshaled their squadrons in defense of the most unholy villainous iniquity the sun ever saw. Mr. Stevens, their Vice President, declared that the Confederacy*

rested upon slavery as the very corner stone of the structure in which human chattelism was to be forever continued; and in the opposition to all this the fact is not to be concealed that the triumph of the North must result in the liberation of our race.

For the first time, then, we are called to our liberty; to show our patriotism, our love of country and our love of our race. We are called upon to shoulder the musket in defense of all we hold dear as men, and by all the memories which cluster around our fathers and brethren of 1776 and 1812. The Government needs our services. It is in a death grapple with human bondage and the lords of the lash. It calls us to its aid. Many of our brethren have heard the call and have gone—they have met the foe on many bloody fields and have exhibited the same dauntless courage and heroism that has ever animated our, when liberty was the boon for which they were contending, whether on the dock of the ship or meeting death on the fiery ramparts of Fort Wagner; on the prairie of Fort Scott, or around the trenches of Port Hudson. Our men have shown to the world that they loved liberty and were willing to lay down their lives in its defense. The Government calls upon us, who have not gone, to go; and we tell you if you want to be respected, you must fight; if you wish social position, you must fight; if you wish political rights, you must fight. A class of men, or a people who are unwilling to strike a blow for their freedom when an opportunity like the present is offered, are unworthy of it. God gives to all oppressed nations an hour in their history when they can be free if they will; that hour, for us is striking now, and ere the sound dies upon the air let us be ready to rise and embrace it. Shakespeare declared that

There is a tide in the affairs of men,
Which, taken at its flood, leads on to fortune;
Omitted, all the voyage of our lives;
Is bound in shallows and in miseries.
We must take the current when it serves
Or lose our venture.

By embracing the present opportunity we can wipe out the stain which ages of oppression has fixed upon us, and win a name for ourselves of which our children will not be shamed.

Authority has been given to Mr. Henry Barns to raise, in Michigan, a regiment of colored men. He has made all the necessary arrangements and commenced recruiting.

The Government has made provision for your acceptance, and every assurance is given by the Hon. Secretary of War, and by our Senators and members of Congress, that a law shall be passed at the next session putting our regiment upon the same footing, as to pay and bounties, as all the white regiments.

Are you ready in this hour of the Nation's peril to lend your aid against the enemies of human freedom and free principles? If so, enroll your names, and, like the Greek or the Pole, or Italian or Hungarian, swear that you will never be content till all your race are free. The richest legacy we can leave our children will be the remembrance of the fact that we fought that they might be free; and should the noblest effort we can now put forth should be to sustain Abraham Lincoln's proclamation, scatter to the winds the false assertion that we will not fight, and win a name is history of which we will be proud.

Colored men of Michigan! A glorious future is before us—will you accept? Will you vindicate your own manhood? Will you give the lie to the base calumniators of our kind, and swear that in defense of this, our native land, our inherent right to Life and Liberty, we will

"Strike till the last armed fox expires,
Strike for our altars and our fires,
Strike for the green graves of our Sires,
God and our native land!"

WILLIAM WEBB
BENJ. CLARK. SR.,
REV. R.A. JOHNSON,
RICHARD GORDON
DR. JOS. FERGUSON,
CAPT. R.L CULLEN,
CHAS W. THOMPSON,
GEO. DEBAPTISTE,
ROBERT PELHAM,
JOHN D. RICHARDS,
Colored men of Detroit.[51]

The 1st Michigan Colored Regiment made its public debut on October 11, 1863, with a detachment of the regiment marching down the streets of Detroit. The 114 soldiers who filled its ranks were wearing the Union blue

George DeBaptiste, born in Fredericksburg, Virginia, in 1816, became a prominent abolitionist and conductor on the Underground Railroad in Detroit. He played a key role in aiding escaped slaves and advocating for African American rights before his death in 1875. *Historical Society of Pennsylvania.*

attire and were armed with Austrian Lorenz muskets. It was said by the older men that they showed good proficiency in drill, marching on beat to the drum much like veterans. The men were in good spirits, disciplined and ready to honor the state of Michigan like the regiment before them. Overall, their first public march was spectacle, drawing much positive attention to the newly formed regiment.[52]

Earlier that month, the citizens of Detroit got an early peek at what was to come when musicians were marching around Jefferson Avenue and Woodbridge, each with his own instrument, marching while playing in sync with one another. These musicians were playing melodies to a group of young boys aged nine and under, who enjoyed the tunes.[53]

On October 12, 1863, an evening war meeting took place at the Colored Baptist Church on Croghan Street. Colonel Sylvester Larned and John D. Richards attended, but the keynote address was delivered by Reverend

Mr. Hunting, who spoke on "The Duty of the Colored Men in the Present Emergency of the Country." A newspaper announcement urged, "Let ever Colored citizen of Detroit and vicinity attend. Be prompt at the hour. Let it be seen that every colored man feels a patriotic interest in the passing events and is ready and anxious to do his whole duty to his country and himself, to help crush the existing rebellion." Similar gatherings were happening across the state, contributing to a rise in enlistment among colored men.[54]

About three hundred local civilians came out to Camp Ward for a religious service on October 25, 1863. Reverend Mr. Inglis of Detroit's Tabernacle Church led the services. The *Advertiser & Tribune* wrote that the chief attraction of the exercises was the singing. It was "congregational in the truest sense, and, though not accompanied by the role of the grand old organ or the well-trained voices of the choir, was none the less solemn or sincere." In this regiment there were several musicians, and it was a goal of the commanders to supply them with the tools needed to perform to keep the men in good spirits. Religious services such as this one were held nearly every Sunday afternoon following the success of this gathering.[55]

With the regiment now having been through a variety of drills, the men held their first dress parade. While still new to the role of the soldier, the men carried themselves quite handsomely. Their eagerness to strive to learn more quickly put them on the path to equality with experienced regiments. Dress parades at Camp Ward attracted many spectators each afternoon. Having the citizens of Michigan visit the camp in person greatly helped to defeat the negative and false narrative being portrayed by papers like the *Free Press*. The *Advertiser & Tribune* wrote:

> *Those who have scolded at the idea of raising a "nigger regiment" in Michigan, and sneered at its beginnings, will have their notions considerably modified if they will visit the camp at 5 o'clock some afternoon. Those engaged in the riot last spring would tremble in their boots at the sight of the glittering army of steel, as firmly held in swarthy hands as ever the sword of vengeance was grasped by the down-trodden Greek or the freedom-loving mountaineers of Switzerland.*[56]

After facing continuous criticism from the *Detroit Free Press*, Barns gave several fact-addressing statements through his paper, the *Detroit Advertiser & Tribune*. In his October 30 1863, statement, he included the reasons for raising Michigan's colored regiment. The first was to give the colored citizens of the area "an opportunity to vindicate their patriotism and bravery." The second reason was that by raising this regiment, it would avoid a draft in the city of Detroit, Wayne County and the state of Michigan. He further added that no regiment started in Detroit, except the 24th Michigan Infantry, had progress as rapidly as the 1st Michigan Colored Regiment.[57]

Three companies of the regiment attended a religious service at Congress Street Baptist Church on the morning of November 1, 1863. The march to the church brought much positive attention, noticeably to their steadfast proficiency in drill. Following this gathering, another service, with several hundred spectators in attendance, was held at Camp Ward, where Reverend S. Hunting of Congress Street Baptist Church officiated the service. At the conclusion of the service, the 1st Michigan Colored Regiment held a dress parade, and the men went through a variety of maneuvers showcasing their skills. The audience was impressed by the progress of the soldiers under the training of their military instructor, Captain William T. Bennett.[58]

Just as much as the environment of a colored regiment was new to the men who enlisted into the regiment, it was also new to those white officers who were commissioned to lead it. This was the first time nearly all the officers and staff were working with colored men in the army. It took some getting used to, as not all of the officers and staff grew up around colored men. One example is James Benjamin Franklin Curtis, who was an enlisted white hospital steward for the 1st Michigan Colored Regiment. After getting to Camp Ward to muster in with his new regiment, Curtis wrote home to his wife notifying her of his arrival. In his letter, he said that several things were to be considered with his new position, the first being that "the rest of the Non commissioned Staff are Niggers."[59]

Lieutenant Colonel William T. Bennett (October 1, 1836–March 10, 1910). Later in the war, he was promoted to colonel of the 33rd USCT after demonstrating strong leadership during the war. He passed away in 1910 and is buried at Los Angeles National Cemetery in Los Angeles, California. *Maurice Imhoff.*

Through the many letters of Dr. Curtis, it is very noticeable that the derogatory term of the colored soldiers being referred to as "niggers" is quickly removed from his vocabulary. It is perhaps due to his new brotherhood and understanding/perspective of the colored population that he never had prior to his enlistment. Spending nearly every day with colored men, Dr. Curtis gained much respect and new friendships with the colored soldiers. It would only be when Dr. Curtis became agitated in a few more letters later in his service, such as when the soldiers lost his dog in transit, that the term was used again. The surgeon quickly gained respect for the soldiers, writing, "I will say that if these boys have to that they will fight in such a manner as to cast no disgrace upon Michigan men!"[60]

The colored men also gained a deep respect and brotherhood bond for their white comrades. Dr. Curtis wrote that as far as he had "heard that the men say that they have the best officers of any regiment and all feel the confidence in their Officer that is required to make good soldiers, & I heard one of them say that they would never run until their officers do! Which I do not think will be very soon."[61]

One of the nation's most famous abolitionists, Sojourner Truth, was greatly invested in supporting the recruitment of Michigan's colored regiment. On November 23, 1863, she visited the men of the 1st Michigan Colored Infantry at Camp Ward. Arriving at eleven o'clock, the carriage stopped in front of Lieutenant Colonel Bennett's quarters with "boxes and packages for the boys." Truth had brought gifts and food for the regiment from the citizens of Battle Creek. The *Advertiser & Tribune* noted that Truth "carries not only a tongue of fire but a heart of love." Colonel Bennett then ordered the regiment to form up "in their best." She gave a speech and formally presented the gifts. The men cheered enthusiastically concluding her speech. Then, for over an hour, she met individually with a number of the soldiers.[62]

I Sell the Shadow to Support the Substance.
SOJOURNER TRUTH.

Sojourner Truth (1797–1883) was a renowned abolitionist and women's rights advocate, born into slavery in New York but freed in 1827. She became famous for her powerful speeches, including the iconic "Ain't I a Woman?" address, and worked tirelessly for the rights of African Americans and women throughout her life. This photo shows her in 1864. *Library of Congress.*

The following day, Truth again addressed the regiment, promising continued support and speaking of their duty as soldiers of the cross during a speech. A large white crowd had also gathered to hear the speech. In her autobiography, Truth printed a song she said she wrote for the 1st Michigan Colored Infantry. This song modifies the lyrics to "John Brown's

Body" ("Battle Hymn of the Republic") and is similar to a song written for the 1st Arkansas Colored Regiment.[63]

The following is the song composed by Sojourner Truth during the war and sung by her in Detroit and Washington:

"The Valiant Soldiers"
Tune.—"John Brown."

We are the valiant soldiers who've 'listed for the war;
We are fighting for the Union, we are fighting for the law;
We can shoot a rebel farther than a white man ever saw,
As we go marching on.

Chorus.—Glory, glory, hallelujah! Glory, glory, hallelujah!
Glory, glory, hallelujah, as we go marching on.

Look there above the center, where the flag is waving bright;
We are going out of slavery, we are bound for freedom's light;
We mean to show Jeff Davis how the African can fight,
As we go marching on.—Chorus.

We are done with hoeing cotton, we are done with hoeing corn;
We are colored Yankee soldiers as sure as you are born.
When massa hears us shouting, he will think 'tis Gabriel's horn,
As we go marching on.—Chorus.

They will have to pay us wages, the wages of their sin;
They will have to bow their foreheads to their colored kith and kin;
They will have to give us house-room, or the roof will tumble in,
As we go marching on.—Chorus.

We hear the proclamation, massa, hush it as you will;
The birds will sing it to us, hoping on the cotton hill;
The possum up the gum tree couldn't keep it still,
As he went climbing on.—Chorus.

Father Abraham has spoken, and the message has been sent;
The prison doors have opened, and out the prisoners went
To join the sable army of African descent,
As we go marching on.—Chorus.[64]

[For the Chicago Tribune.]

Sojourner Truth, and "The Only Son of His Mother."

Not far from the city of Battle Creek, Michigan, resides one J. A. ——, a well-known "conservative" of what peculiar type it is difficult to determine; but one thing is certain, he does not like an abolitionist.

A few weeks since, Sojourner Truth was preparing to visit her friends of the 1st Michigan regiment of colored men, and was seeking aid to pay her expenses. She met J. A. ——, in a store, and appealed to him, but without success. Some conversation ensued—enough to reveal to the shrewd old lady his character. He turned to leave, and she called out, "Who be you?"

"I am the *only son* of my mother," was the response.

"Thank God, there are no more," said Sojourner.

It is needless to add that the "conservative" left abou that time. Pass this around.

Newspaper article describing an interaction between Truth and a white man. *Library of Michigan.*

As the months progressed through the recruiting process, recruits continued to make their way to Camp Ward in Detroit from across the region. The Evansville, Indiana newspaper reported that it had about forty colored men making their way through their city heading for Detroit. Many nearby residents of Detroit were still skeptical of the thought of enlisted colored soldiers, especially still reading negative articles about the regiment from the *Detroit Free Press*. To help get a personal understanding for themselves, civilians would often visit Camp Ward to watch the drills or dress parades taking place. On November 24, 1863, approximately sixty new recruits were mustered in and given their uniforms. The following day, these same new recruits, mixed among several companies, were drilling as efficiently with their head high as the previous enlisted men. One of the local citizens spectating the drills, initially doubtful of the regiment, left Camp Ward fully convinced of their ability as soldiers. The *Detroit Advertiser & Tribune* noted "their firm and steady step in the clean, bright appearance of their arms and uniforms, were calculated to create a favorable impression in the prejudiced mind."[65]

Chapter 7

Camp Ward

The camp for the regiment, known as Camp Ward, was located on land that was originally a farm owned by A. Campau and used as a training site for the 5th Michigan Cavalry. This location was east of Elmwood Cemetery and extended to Joseph Campau Street. It ran north to Clinton Street and south to Croghan Street. The camp was under the direction of Captain Orson W. Bennett. While no picture of Camp Ward is known to exist, descriptions provide an idea of what the property looked like. The ground had good drainage, and several structures had been constructed, including a commissary store/quartermaster's department, guardhouse, sutler's shop and several buildings for company quarters. There was no fence around the property, but the guardhouse provided a military feel.[66]

Each of the company quarters were built of wood and contained two cook stoves with all the necessary accoutrements. The kitchen was the only room in the company quarters that had floors. Forks and knives were kept in racks, plates on shelves and tin cups on nails on the wall. Provisions were stored in a larder and doled out for the daily rations the men received. Despite what the letter outlining the regulations for the regiment might suggest, the enlisted men were given regular army rations. The officers' quarters were comfortable but could not have been considered luxurious. The *Detroit Advertiser & Tribune* noted that "the whole appearance of the camp indicated neatness and order."[67]

Civil War training camps were essential in transforming civilian recruits into disciplined soldiers capable of withstanding the harsh realities of wartime service. At these camps, soldiers learned the "School of the Soldier," which consisted of fundamental military drills, formations and the basics of maintaining discipline and order within the ranks. Through daily practice, men became adept at close-order drill and marching in formation, which were crucial for effective maneuvering on the battlefield. The repetitive drills taught recruits how to act in unison, respond to commands and work cohesively as a unit—skills that could mean life or death in the chaos of combat. This rigorous preparation was vital, as many soldiers were new to military life and had to rapidly adjust to its demands.[68]

Beyond mastering drills and formations, training camps introduced recruits to the conditions they would encounter on the front lines. Camps were organized to simulate the living conditions soldiers would face in the field, exposing them to life in barracks or tents and the daily routines of camp life, including hygiene practices, cooking and guard duty. This exposure helped the men acclimate to the hardships of soldiering, from enduring adverse weather to coping with limited supplies. Such experiences were intended to build resilience, allowing soldiers to adapt to the challenging environments they would encounter at the front. Military camps also instilled the importance of following strict routines and obeying orders, laying the foundation for discipline and efficiency in battle.[69]

A significant part of training focused on weapons handling, as recruits learned to load, aim and fire their rifles under various conditions. For many soldiers, especially those with little or no prior experience with firearms, this was a critical skill to master. Instructors drilled men in marksmanship and taught them how to maintain and care for their weapons, ensuring that they could operate efficiently under pressure. Bayonet training was also included, preparing soldiers for the brutal close combat that often characterized Civil War battles. These skills, reinforced through repetition and drill, helped ensure that soldiers could face the enemy with confidence and cohesion. Training camps thus played a crucial role in not only equipping men with technical skills but also in building the mental and physical toughness required for sustained warfare.[70]

Articles from the time of organization tell of the schedule followed at Camp Ward: "5:00 Reveille, 5:00–6:00 Policing, 6:00 Sick Call, 7:00 Breakfast, 8:00 Drill for noncommissioned officers, 9:00 Guard mounting, 10:00 Squad drill, 11:30 Recall, 12:00 Lunch, 2:00 Drill for noncommissioned officers, 5:00 Dress Parade, 8:00 Tattoo, 8:30 Taps."[71]

While no official records explain the namesake behind the military new instillation, Camp Ward was likely named after local Detroit abolitionist and businessman "Captain" Eder Brock Ward (1811–1875). He was often involved in hosting gatherings to raise awareness about the evil of slavery with hopes to gain more local activist. In 1856, following violence in Kansas known as "Bleeding Kansas," Ward donated $10,000 toward the abolitionist movement to "Free Kansas" and would also go on to fund the freedom of escaped slaves in Detroit, whose freedom was on the line when the bounty hunters came for them. Among other things, he was Detroit's first millionaire. Colonel Henry Barns was associated with Ward through Ward's involvement in the local abolitionist newspapers through the news.[72]

In late November 1863, the colored citizens of Detroit and surrounding areas gathered for a large and enthusiastic meeting, joined by a portion of the colored regiment, to confront the negative press bashing their efforts. The target of their outrage was clear: the *Detroit Free Press*. In a bold and uncompromising set of resolutions, the community voiced its collective indignation and reaffirmed its unwavering commitment to justice, service and freedom. They began by naming the enemy plainly: "an unscrupulous pro-slavery newspaper, published in the city of Detroit," which, along with "a gang of unprincipled and hungry speculators," had sought to defame Colonel Henry Barns and rob colored volunteers of their rightful bounties. The meeting declared, "We recognize the *Detroit Free Press* as a ancient and persistent enemy of the colored man—seeking by every means in its power to keep him in, or if let out, to drag him back to the galling chains of slavery." This was no sudden betrayal; the paper had long vilified people of color, "always willing to take up any lie, or pervert any truth," in order to "accomplish their hellish purpose of keeping us degraded."[73]

The resolutions struck directly at the paper's hypocrisy. In earlier days, the *Free Press* had "abused us as being a pest in this community," even calling for legal measures to "correct the growing evil." Yet now, with the nation desperate for men to fight, the paper had "fallen in love with the negro," becoming "his special advocate and defender," filling its columns with hollow praise while doing more than any other force "to keep men from our regiment." The citizens were particularly upset by a recent false report in the *Free Press* claiming that colored soldiers had been thrown into the guardhouse at Camp Ward for being "about to abscond with their bounties." The resolution condemned this as a "base and wicked calumny" meant to discredit the regiment and dissuade enlistment. It was, they declared, "put forth for the purpose of injuring the regiment and Colonel Barns." They also rejected the *Free Press*'s unfounded attacks on Lieutenant Colonel Bennett, who was working closely with Barns to lead the regiment.[74]

The resolutions then turned to another group of saboteurs—"money sharks" who lured soldiers to transfer their enlistment to other states for bribes. These "robbers," they wrote, were "too mean to risk their own cowardly carcasses upon the battlefield," and instead sought profit from the bodies not just of colored men, "but of women and children" as well. Yet amid these attacks, the assembled citizens voiced strong and loyal support for Colonel Barns. "We recognize in Col. Barns an old and tried friend," they wrote, a man who had faithfully advocated for them and treated the men with "marked kindness in camp." Barns had helped many soldiers secure their full bounty before bonds were even finalized. For this, he had earned their trust. "We stand by him," they resolved, "he has been true to us so far, we believe he will continue so."[75]

The final resolution resounded with moral clarity and patriotic fervor. Framing the war as a struggle "between Freedom on one hand and Slavery on the other," they affirmed that "every pulsation of our hearts, every sympathy of our beings, every aspiration of our souls" called them to action. They were ready, they declared, "to strike a blow for our own elevation, and, like the Pole or the Hungarian or Greek, to sacrifice home and life, if need be, in defense of liberty." Declaring before God and country, they resolved that "no influence shall alienate love of our country, or the determination to fight till all are free."[76]

Chapter 8

A Grand Southern Tour

On December 3, 1863, the 1st Michigan Colored Infantry was furnished with instruments and formed a fifteen-member regimental band. Though only having their instruments for two days, the brass band played well during a march two days later. This new band was funded by music composer J. Henry Whittemore with a donation of $528. The band contained several coronets, other brass instruments, cymbals and two drums. Within a matter of weeks, they were being praised by newspapers for their playing ability. Just a few days after the band was formed, about 250 men of the regiment began a tour through the state organized by Colonel Barns. They traveled along the Michigan Southern Railroad in a sufficient number of freight cars outfitted for the men, while the officers rode in a regular passenger car. Barns arranged the trip to show off the regiment, encourage recruitment and increase support for colored regiments. During this time, the 1st Michigan Colored Infantry visited Ypsilanti, Ann Arbor, Jackson, Marshall, Kalamazoo, Dowagiac, Cassopolis and Niles. At each location, the regiment was greeted by a crowd of people, both white and Black. They were typically fed a meal and performed maneuvers in a dress parade, and then the band played while marching into the town.[77]

On the bright morning of December 8, under what was described as "a regular spring atmosphere," the 1st Michigan Colored Regiment prepared to embark on its grand southern tour. Before boarding the excursion train, the regiment marched proudly through several of Detroit's main streets, the beat of their steps matched by the stirring music of the regimental

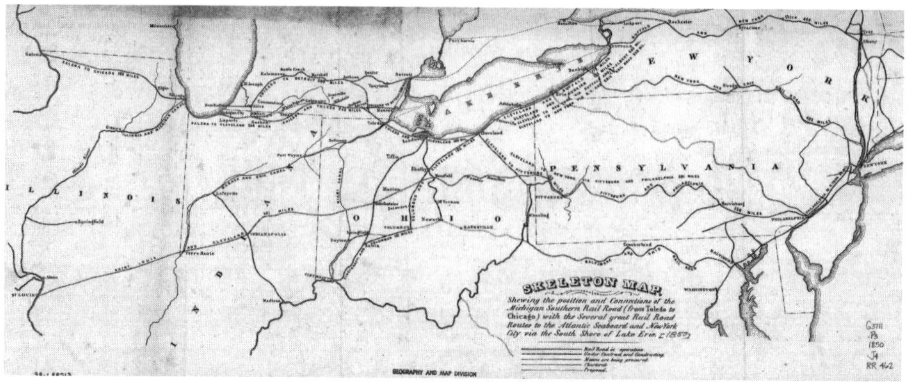

An 1850 map of the Michigan Southern Railroad. *Library of Congress.*

band. Along the way, the regiment paused in front of the residence of Mr. Rice, the superintendent of the Central Railroad, where the band performed a few favorite pieces. Shortly after ten o'clock, the train stood ready. As the regiment boarded, a loud and prolonged hurrah erupted from the "vast assemblage" that had gathered to witness their departure. The music from the regimental band continued as the train pulled out, and a short ride brought the soldiers to the junction, where a large crowd of passengers and spectators were assembled. There, a few lively numbers from the band reignited the cheers of onlookers. Along the route, every station and house became a stage for celebration—people waved, shouted and competed in enthusiasm.[78]

At Ypsilanti, men and women filled the streets, eager for a glimpse of the colored soldiers. There was a rush to pass refreshments through the train windows, a showering of care from sweethearts, friends and neighbors, all gathered in the hundreds "to pay their respects to the 'boys.'" The entire experience mirrored the emotional farewells seen when a regiment departed for war. Even local business in Ypsilanti seemed to pause, as the large community turnout turned the moment into a civic spectacle. As the train finally pulled away, with the battalion leaving to continue its venture, it was met once again with loud, heartfelt cheers, a clear signal that these men were not just leaving—they were leaving honored.[79]

When the regiment arrived at its next stop in Ann Arbor, the welcome was overwhelming. "It was gratifying," a correspondent in the *Detroit Advertiser & Tribune* wrote, "to see the immense concourse of people that had turned out." The depot grounds were packed with citizens, both Black and white, to such an extent that it became "quite difficult for the men to get off the

Built in 1860 on the southwest corner of Main and Washington, the Italianate-style Hangsterfer's Block housed a confectionery shop and, by 1863, the First National Bank on the ground floor. Its third-floor hall became a lively cultural center, hosting lectures, plays, dances and social events catered by Mr. Jacob Hangsterfer. *Ann Arbor District Library.*

cars." In about fifteen minutes, the soldiers finally disembarked and got into marching formation. With precision and dignity, they proceeded through the heart of the city—up Detroit Street, then Ann Street and down Main Street—until they reached Hangsterfer's Hall.[80]

There, the regiment stacked arms and was treated to a generous and elegant meal. Three long tables stretched the length of the hall, "well filled with the good things of this life," and the meal was noted to have been served with "full justice." A local committee—composed of citizens including Judge Lawrence, C.B. Thompson, O.M. Martin, L. Davis, William A. Hatch, Luther Dodge and William McCreary—had worked quickly and efficiently to organize the welcome. With only three hours' notice of the regiment's arrival, several gentlemen immediately placed orders for refreshments, gathered contributions and managed to fund the entire event without delay. The reception deeply moved the regiment. The men expressed pride in the treatment they had received, and the Ann Arbor residents expressed their admiration in turn.[81]

After the meal, the regiment reformed ranks once more and marched to the commons, where it performed military drills and maneuvers. The crowd responded with enthusiastic applause, impressed by the soldiers' discipline and professionalism. "They certainly did excellently," the *Tribune*'s observer noted, "and were loudly applauded." Perhaps most significantly, the visit marked a shift in public sentiment. "Even thus far a manifest change is perceptible," the article noted, referring to the growing respect and enthusiasm for colored soldiers. New recruits were already beginning to come forward, inspired by the honor and conduct of the regiment.[82]

The largest stop was in Jackson on December 9, 1863. The regiment planned to arrive at nine o'clock but was delayed until midnight, as the first freight train they boarded was too heavily loaded, causing them to stay in Ann Arbor awhile longer. The regiment then arrived in Jackson at about one o'clock in the morning. Unfortunately, the supper that was planned for the regiment at the Marion House had to be canceled due to this late arrival. Through the generosity of Mrs. Blair, wife of Governor Austin Blair, the regiment was able to use this large hall for sleeping quarters. The local provost marshal, Captain Barry, was able to supply every man of the regiment (except the band) with blankets to make their short stay comfortable.[83]

However, the late arrival did not stop the locals from treating them to a heartfelt meal. With some help cooking from the soldiers of the regiment, the first company was treated to a breakfast a five o'clock in the morning, with the remaining companies to follow. Following breakfast, at about 9:30 a.m., the men regiment formed up into line to make their way to the governor's home. They then marched down the local roads to his personal residence not far away on Lansing Avenue. Along the route, the streets were filled with local spectators, who loudly cheered for the Black soldiers. Admiring their clean and disciplined appearance, the men were handsomely complimented. A reporter for the *Detroit Advertiser & Tribune* said that he did not hear a single reproachful or disparaging remark made in reference to them.[84]

What made this visit to the people of Jackson so special? This community was known to be a strong and passionate abolitionist city, one of the most not only in Michigan but also the entire country. On July 6, 1854, a large gathering with reportedly five thousand to ten thousand people in attendance took place in Jackson under a grove of Michigan's winding oak trees. This gathering, with the primary goal of stopping the spread of slavery in America, was later to be named "Under the Oaks." A local newspaper editor and abolitionist Charles DeLand, who later would enlist in the war, sent more than one thousand invites across Michigan for the mass convention. Citizens fed up with the country's political climate and ready for a new path came in droves until there was no longer standing room in Jackson's Bronson Hall. The convention was then moved to an outdoor location nearby prominently known as Morgan's Forty.[85]

A committee made up of sixteen men met separately on the corner of Jackson's Franklin Street and Second Street. Now in a quieter setting, they produced several resolutions. Notably, one resolution called for the immediate repeal of the Kansas-Nebraska Act. The recently passed 1854 law sparked much of the energy that brought attendees to this convention. The law allowed settlers of Kansas and Nebraska to choose for themselves whether to allow slavery in such states. This issue was directly addressed in the gathering's invite:

> *All of our fellow citizens, without reference to political association, who think that the time has arrived for a union to protect liberty from being overthrown and downtrodden, to assemble in mass convention on the 6th of July next at Jackson...* [calling on citizens to] *take such measure as shall be best to concentrate the popular sentiment of this state against the encroachment of slave power.*[86]

The committee also put forth a slate of candidates who openly opposed slavery in the United States. It was also this committee that agreed to formally adopt the name "Republican." For this reason, the visit of the 1st Michigan Colored Regiment was special—to have a regiment only nine years later comprising Black men and boys marching through the same city where the party to lead the effort to end slavery in American once and for all was born.[87]

Now having marched through the city, the 1st Michigan Colored Regiment arrived at Governor Austin Blair's residence and positioned itself in an open area nearby. The officers then put the regiment through a variety of drills showcasing their well-trained group to those in attendance, which included Governor Blair, Colonel Loomis, provost marshal Captain Barry, Dr. Baker of the 21st Michigan Regiment and the large number of attendees, with a noticeable number being woman. At the conclusion of the drill, the regiment was formed into its hollow square formation, after which Lieutenant Colonel William T. Bennett introduced Governor Blair. "Michigan's War Governor" made the following remarks:

Officers And Soldiers: I find my position in your square somewhat new. Is the first time that I ever saw a battalion of colored soldiers together, and I, together with, the vast concourse you seeing surrounding you, feel proud of your general bearing. The people of this country are beginning to feel interested in you. They are proud to see colored soldiers banded together to fight for a country that has herefore promised much, but has never accomplished a great deal for the colored race. It has done much for everyone but you. That feeling to his last being dispelled, and the time will come when the world at all recognize is that the constitution of our country means what it says, that every man shall enjoy life, liberty, and pursuit of happiness. [Prolonged applause.] *I hope you will be able to fight so as to put the country under an obligation to you, your colored brethren and arms in South Carolina have borne a conspicuous part in reestablishing the banner of our glorious country upon the ramparts of Fort Wagner, have helped to plant the stars and stripes where they would never again be removed by the hand of treason.* [Cheers.]

Take courage then, do your duty nobly. Your noble dusky brethren have indeed won for themselves the richest laurels on mini a battlefield. By these deeds you will secure the goodwill of all, and a prominent place in the country. Already there are thousands of colored men rushing to arms in their countries cause, and in a few months, I verily believe, there will be upwards of 100,000 colored men in the ranks. Imagine, if you can, 100,000 bayonets in the hands of dusky soldiers, and then see if the Copperheads will dare to revile the brave soldiers of the Union. [Cheers.]

Quite recently the country has heard the glad tidings of the series of successes in Tennessee. The flag of our country has been painted upon the high pinnacle of Lookout Mountain, in the very heart of the so called Southern Confederacy. In the midst of a country where your brethren have been held bondage. The flag placed there may be looked up to, floating from the eminence, as an ornament to future generations. The great Proclamation of Freedom is being made a fact. It was written about a year ago, that all men held bondage in those States remaining in rebellion up to a certain time, should hereafter be free. Daily we are witnessing the beneficial and holy effects of that document. Victory over the entire armed host of the rebellion is not far distant, and foreign governments are beginning to recognize the fact. The British lion, that a year ago was endeavoring to hem us in, preparatory to swallowing us whole, is now as calm as a sucking dove. The Frenchman, whose ideas were fast becoming wedded in favor of the rebels, is changing his tune, and now that he felt

> *secure in his newly-effected foothold in Mexico, he is quite willing to let us alone.*
>
> *Learn thoroughly the duties of a soldier. Take care to be manly and well informed upon your duties and responsibilities. Learn well the character you have assumed. Observe good and orderly regulations. Avoid vicious and dissipated habits, and all immoral practices. Obey your officers, and the result will be that you will come out the contest better informed of what you really are, and what you can do. Remember that you have a dignity to maintain. We have committed to your care the flag of our country. That you will fight for it no one doubts, and if perchance any of you should fall, there will be a consolation that you will find honorable graves. It is my earnest wish that you may escape unharmed, and that you may be able to return to your families. Such shall be my prayers, as well as of all those who love their country. Hoping to see you again ere you depart for the rest of war, I bid you goodbye.*[88]

Following Governor Blair's speech, the audience cheered, and the men gave three cheers to their state's leader. The regiment went then went through a few more military maneuvers before marching back into town for dinner. The men left Jackson for Marshall at about 1:30 p.m. At each way station on the route to Marshall, the local citizenry came in large numbers to greet the regiment and were very disappointed that the men did not get off to visit.[89]

Arriving in Marshall, the men were greeted by the town's mayor, Charles Cameron, along with several community leaders who then led them through the town. For several hours, the 1st Michigan Colored Infantry Regiment drilled in the area. Now approaching five o'clock in the afternoon, the regiment formed into their hollow square formation in front of the Facey House. W.H. Brown gave an influential speech to the regiment, giving them compelling advice, which was interrupted several times from the regiment cheering in excitement. The citizens of Marshall were very supportive and joyous about the visit of the colored regiment. During the evening, at six o'clock, the men made their way inside the Facey House, where the citizens helped to provide them with food. Nearing seven o'clock in the evening, the 1st Michigan Colored Regiment left Marshall for Kalamazoo.[90]

At about midnight, the regiment arrived in Kalamazoo. Unfortunately, upon arrival, the officers had learned that accommodations had not been made for the men. However, that didn't stop local Black community organizations from helping. A large local hall was tendered for them, fitting

Built by Andrew Mann in 1835, this structure is recognized as the first brick building in Calhoun County. Known originally as Mann's Hotel, the National House accommodated travelers passing through Marshall and served as a venue for political and community events. Over time, it took on different names, including the Acker House and Facey House, and was even repurposed for industrial uses, such as a wagon and windmill factory. Still standing today, the two-story, low-gabled building has been restored to its original design and functions once again as an inn. *John Garman.*

about half the regiment inside, and the other half were able to stay inside a few local churches. In the morning, the commanding officers learned that Mayor Allen Potter had given the responsibility of taking care of the troops to the city marshal. However, with the city marshal apathetic about taking care of the troops' visit, the responsibility passed to Frederick Wilkinson, state agent of the U.S. Sanitary Commission. At nine o'clock in the morning, the regiment was served a filling breakfast. The regiment stayed in Kalamazoo through the early part of the day. Later that afternoon, before three o'clock, Lieutenant Governor Charles Sedgwick May gave a cheerful speech to the 1st Michigan Colored Regiment. Following the speech, the regiment was served a filling dinner from the community thanks to local ladies of the city, Lieutenant Governor May, Judge Wells and others.[91]

A reporter for the *Detroit Advertiser & Tribune* noted:

> *Your readers in the city can form no conception of the magnitude of the reception given to the colored soldiers, and the excursion has, and will continue to work in earnest and visible change in the sentiments of the*

people in reference to colored soldiers, and it is expression of nine-tenths of the people along the line that the regiment will be speedily be filled.

Just so far on the tour, the regiment has already secured several troops—five in Ypsilanti, thirty in Ann Arbor, fifteen in Jackson and several from Marshall. Their fine appearance, discipline and soldierly manner continuously brought compliments to Lieutenant Colonel Bennett, who was very much the men's drill instructor. Following dinner, the regiment left the city of Kalamazoo around 4:30 p.m. for Niles.[92]

On December 11 at about nine o'clock at night, the 1st Michigan Colored Regiment arrived in Niles. The regiment was greeted by a salute of more than thirty guns, bonfires and cheers when the men arrived at the Niles depot. The majority of those gathered were people of color. However, there were several white citizens who came to see the occasion. The regiment deboarded the train and made its way down the local streets to Kellogg's Hall. The building's proprietor, Mr. A.B. Chipman, generously donated the space for the regiment's stay that night for just fifteen dollars. The officers and reporters stayed at the popular Bond House. In the morning, the regiment was treated to a "substantial breakfast" thanks to local colored citizens and Chaplain Waring. A warm batch of coffee was also prepared with the food. However, the men had a very difficult time finding enough cups to drink with. At about nine o'clock, the regiment marched through the streets of Niles, drawing a large audience. After drilling, they formed into their hollow square formation and received an address by Niles Mayor Henry M. Dean and local *Freeman* newspaper editor Thomas H. Glenn. Later that day, the regiment held a dress parade where George M. Dewey, editor and publisher of the *Niles Enquirer*, delivered a prolonged speech.[93]

Main Street looking east, Kalamazoo, circa 1860s. Photographed by S.C. Baldwin. *Kalamazoo Public Library.*

Not everyone in Niles was in favor of the colored regiment's visit. In fact, some of the area Copperheads were looking forward to mocking the appearance of what they labeled the "Nigger Regiment." To their surprise, the regiment was disciplined and did exceptionally well with the military tactics of the period. These Copperheads became so impressed that they admitted their change of opinion on Michigan's colored regiment, and some even went on to speak highly of the men. That night, the colored ladies of Niles held a grand ball for the 1st Michigan. The gathering was well attended, and the soldiers attended in good numbers. Following the ball, a large and energized war meeting was held at Kellogg's Hall to help recruit more volunteers for the regiment. Many men did enlist in the regiment following the close of the meeting.[94]

The next morning, the 1st Michigan Colored Regiment had its physical abilities put to the test, leaving at six o'clock on foot to march to Cassopolis. The men of the regiment were "exultant" learning of the plan of the march, entertaining the idea of a march "even into Dixie." Making their way to Cassopolis, the men faced little difficulty handling the sixteen-mile march. The local farmers who saw the regiment pass gave the men fruit and shouted

During the American Civil War, "Copperheads" referred to a faction of Northern Democrats who opposed the war and advocated for an immediate peace settlement with the Confederacy. They were often criticized for their anti-war sentiments and accused of being disloyal to the Union cause, which led to tensions with more pro-war factions. The editorial cartoon depicts three exaggerated caricatures of Copperheads approaching Columbia, who is wielding a sword and holding a shield marked "Union." *Library of Congress.*

with excitement. Unfortunately, as the men were half the distance from Cassopolis, rainy weather began to factor into their travel, and the roads became "extremely wet and heavy." The citizens of Cassopolis lent their support for the regiment, providing shelter for them in the local courthouse and even giving the men refreshments after a long, muddy march. The majority of the village's population contributed food and money to support their visit. After an invitation by Reverend Sherwood, the men attended a religious service at the local Presbyterian church. Later that evening, another religious service was held by the regimental chaplain, Willian Waring, at the courthouse where the regiment was quartered.[95]

In the morning, the regiment marched over to the area's fairgrounds for dress parade and drill. Many of the local area residents came out to watch. Following the conclusion of the formation, the regiment formed into its hollow square formation, and Charles Wesley Clisbee gave a speech to the regiment, after which the regiment cheered. These cheers spooked Lieutenant Colonel Bennett's horse, causing it dash into the audience. Bennett, working to protect the women and children from the frantic animal, was thrown roughly to the ground, causing him to dislocate his shoulder. Unfortunately, despite the lieutenant colonel's brave actions, the horse ran into a colored woman and child. With Colonel Bennett and the others being treated, Captain Benjamin of Company took command of the regiment and marched it to its sleeping quarters in the village.[96]

On Monday, December 14, 1863, at about nine o'clock in the morning, the 1st Michigan Colored Regiment was formed up to begin its march to Dowagiac. The weather was not on their side that morning, as there was a heavy snowstorm mixed with high winds. To stay warm, the men of the regiment wrapped their capes around their ears. Before leaving, the men gave three cheers for the citizens of Cassopolis. The regimental brass band played "John Brown's Body," with nearly two hundred men of the regiment joining in on singing the chorus. The citizens cheered them on as they began their ten-mile march to the village of Dowagiac.[97]

This march unfortunately came with sorrow. While on their way, the men learned that Second Sergeant William E. Washington (eighteen years of age) of Company D, who had grown unwell at Niles, had passed away.[98]

Marching for about two hours, the regiment arrived in Dowagiac, where the men had refreshments. Soon after arriving, the men were pleasantly settled into several places. Citizens from surrounding villages who were in the area were unaware of the colored regiment's planned visit and were surprised to see them. A welcoming gathering took place inside the village's

Above: *A Bit of War History: The Recruit*, by Thomas Waterman Wood. *Metropolitan Museum of Art.*

Opposite: The Dowagiac train depot a few years earlier in 1860, from Front Street. *Dowagiac Area History Museum.*

Michigan Central Railroad freight depot, where the regiment was served dinner. This was thanks to Mr. Spencer and Mr. Campbell of the local *Cass County Republican* newspaper, along with the local citizens. With the snowstorm in full effect, the regiment did not hold a dress parade in Dowagiac. Despite this, the *Cass County Republican* reported that "we are assured that they are fully equal to any troops who have been in the service no longer than they." Later that evening, at ten o'clock, the 1st Michigan Colored Regiment, energized from its tour, began its way home to Camp Ward in Detroit.[99]

Overall, the tour was a success. This expedition of southern Michigan secured the support of citizens and gained recruits for the regiment at each location. After the second stop in Ann Arbor, the *Detroit Advertiser & Tribune* stated, "Even thus far a manifest change in perceptible in the general tone of people relative to colored soldiers." By the time the 1st Michigan Colored Regiment reached Kalamazoo alone, it had added more than fifty men to the ranks.[100]

From the Confederacy to the Union Cause

Henry McIntosh, born enslaved on a Kentucky plantation in 1843, certainly has one of the more compelling stories of those enlisted. Initially forced into service as a horse wrangler for the Confederate army when the war broke out in 1861, McIntosh, like many enslaved men, longed for freedom. A horse wrangler was responsible for managing and caring for horses used by the army, particularly in cavalry units or for officers. Their duties included feeding, grooming and saddling, ensuring that the horses were ready for battle or travel. Wranglers also looked after the horses when not in use, including leading them to water and keeping them calm during the chaos of battle. They played a crucial role in maintaining the mobility of mounted troops, artillery units and supply wagons, as horses were essential for transportation during the Civil War.[101]

After several months, McIntosh seized the opportunity to escape from his involvement in the Confederate army, crossing the Ohio River into a free state. Guided by the Underground Railroad, McIntosh made his way north, stopping in Detroit, Michigan. Detroit had a growing African American community, where McIntosh found refuge and hope. He was determined to return to the fight—this time as a free man on the side of the Union. He knew that the struggle to end slavery was far from over, and he wanted to be a part of the effort to liberate those still trapped in bondage. By joining the Union army, he sought not only his personal freedom but also the chance to strike back against the very institution and army that had oppressed him.[102]

On New Year's Eve 1864, Henry McIntosh enlisted in Company G of the 1st Michigan Colored Regiment at twenty-one years old, a regiment whose mission aligned with his own: the defeat of the Confederate forces and the ultimate destruction of the system of slavery. McIntosh, like many other formerly enslaved men, saw military service as a way to fight for freedom and the destruction of slavery. This wasn't just about military victory; it was about justice for millions of enslaved men, women and children who were still suffering in the South. His desire to return to the battlefield as a Union soldier reflected his deep commitment to fighting for the freedom of others.[103]

After the war ended, McIntosh returned to Michigan with the regiment and, shortly after, moved to Lake Forest, Illinois, where he sought new opportunities and built a life for himself. In Lake Forest, McIntosh became a respected member of the community. He married Sarah Martin in 1869 and was a founding member of the African Methodist Episcopal Church, where he maintained a lifelong involvement. After Sarah's death in 1884, he remarried Fannie Davis Freleigh in 1885, and the couple had nine children together. McIntosh worked as a laborer, coachman and gardener and was an active member of the Lake County Soldiers and Sailors

Association. He remained a symbol of resilience and service, living a long life until his death in 1915, remembered as both a Civil War veteran and a community leader.[104]

Ultimately, McIntosh's experience reflected the larger aspirations of African Americans during the Civil War, who saw the Union army not just as a path to personal freedom but also as a force for societal change. For McIntosh, every battle fought against the Confederates was a step toward justice, a way to avenge the years of oppression and bring freedom to those still in chains. He fought not just for himself but for the future of a nation free from slavery.[105]

Chapter 9

Barracks of Injustice

A Call for Dignity at Camp Ward

During the early winter of 1864, cold weather began to affect the regiment. Camp Ward became nearly uninhabitable due to poor conditions. The *Detroit Advertiser & Tribune* expressed its outrage at the poor conditions of the colored soldiers' barracks.[106]

Negros in Michigan During the Civil War, a book written for the centennial of the war, summarized the complaints from the "Journal of the Prosecution of the War." Criticisms of Camp Ward included "no tar paper on the roof, leaky roofs, no flooring, cervices in the side of the buildings large enough to allow for snow drifts, sacks of straw in lieu of beds, and poor ventilation."[107] The *Detroit Advertiser & Tribune* had this to say:

> *The U.S. barracks almost immediately opposite, are constructed with purely with a view to comfort the quarters are all neatly floored, and the roofs and sides are made impervious to water or snow, and ingress and egress to them is made over substantial boardwalks. We cannot see why there should be so much difference between the quarters of white troops and the huts of colored men.*

Reports soon named George W. Lee, the U.S. Army Quartermaster Department's representative in Detroit, as being at fault for this issue. An official investigation into the matter was opened. Nevertheless, there was no doubt through the entire city that Camp Ward had become inhumane for any human being in such a winter climate.[108]

Dr. Charles S. Tripler, surgeon for the U.S. Army, came to Camp Ward to inspect the situation in December after a request from Lieutenant Colonel B.H. Hill, adjutant general in Detroit. After completing an inspection, Dr. Tripler stated:

> *SIR:—I have the honor to report that in compliance with your instructions, I have inspected the barracks occupied by the regiment of colored troops now being raised in the city. The buildings occupied by the rank and file are six in number, each 24 by 12 feet. They are rough, green pine board, without frame, open joints, with a pitch roof also rough boards, but with the joints overlaid. There are no floors. In the center of each building are two ranges of rough boards laid at tables. There is one door midway of the length of each building facing the parade, and a chorus bonding door opening into a small kitchen on the opposite. There are two windows at one end and one window at the other end of the building. The roughest kinds of bunks, three stories high, are arranged along the sides of the building. The men have mixed up a number of these to make them more comfortable. They are furnished with straw, but without bed sacks. There is on the side of some of the buildings a latticed air chimney. The quarters are heated by two stoves each. The roof and sides of the building afford but very imperfect protection against either rain or wind, there is no ventilation, except through the open joints of the boards, and even this is more detrimental than beneficial to the health of the men, while the partial currents of air thus admitted only increased the discomfort of the inmates. The surface of the ground formatting the floor is not even smoothed off, and in wet weather, on such soil, must always be muddy as well tough.*
>
> *The police of these corridors is wretched; the wood for the stoves seemed to be cut with axes inside the rooms and the chips are left scattered over the floor. The men's tables are filthy—the straw in the bunks, I should judge, was never aired or changed. The provisions furnished to the men are good. The quarters of the officers, though furnished with board floors, are in other respects as bad as those of the men.*
>
> *I should recommend all the buildings to be furnished with plated board floors, raised at least eight inches from the ground, the walls to be lined inside; all the joints battened. The roof to be covered with tarred paper and card (composition roof), more windows to be introduced, and such as may be opened at will for ventilation: more rooms to be built so that the men cannot be compelled to eat and sleep in the same apartments: decent*

and comfortable bunks to be pat up and furnished with bedsack: one blanket to a man, is not sufficient to the climate in the winter.

I think for both safety and comfort brick flues should be built for the stove pipes, as it present arranged, in my opinion these quarters are utterly unfit for either officers or men.[109]

U.S. Quartermaster Lee fired back against the claims of the *Detroit Advertiser & Tribune*, sending a letter to the paper that was published by *Detroit Free Press*:

U.S. Quartermasters Office
Detroit. Dec. 23, 1863

To the editors of the Advertiser and Tribune:
Several articles having appeared in your paper within the last few days, closing today with Surgeon Chas. S. Tripler, U.S.A., over his official signature, you will oblige me by allowing a place in your columns of your paper for the following, since you have proclaimed that I am responsible for the state of things at the camp of the colored regiment:

In August I received a letter from the Q.M. General instructions to erect a temporary barracks for the colored regiment which Henry Barnes [sic], *Esq., had the authority to raise, and had which he* [Barns] *proposed to raise in sixty days. You will observe that nearly five months have elapsed, and under no consideration or probability of case could we have expected it to have delayed to this day.*

The men's quarters are 6 in number, 52 by 24, 4 doors and four double windows and each, instead of 2 by 12, and two doors and three windows. Some of the windows have been broken and closed up, and some of the doors also have been closed by the officers or soldiers. I am surprised that the doctor did not in his examination and inspection of these quarters observe the kitchens, that all have floors, 2 windows, and two stoves each, additional to those mentioned, belonging to each building, or that the filth on the table made them appear as unplanned.

I was responsible for the barracks as they were not as they now are, and yet in their present condition (excluding the filth) I appeal to thousands and 10s of thousands of our brave boys and arms whether these quarters are not as good as any furnished encampment of a majority of our regiments while organizing, and far better than are found in the field.

Again, I am not responsible for the condition in which these quarters are kept, or that the men do not have the bed sacks, and if they are not comfortable it is their own fault, as materials have been furnished to make them so, and the only suggestion I can make from their benefit is (since all the material for which it can recruit is exhausted in this State) that they can move to a more congenial clime near of usefulness, for which they were designed, and abundant opportunity afford them to fill their ranks, instead of bringing recruits from the South to transport back at the expense of the government.

Hoping you may find topics of more importance to the public than the gratification of some disappointed individual who has originated this discussion.[110]

To help support his message, Quartermaster Lee also included a letter from Lieutenant Colonel Joseph Rowe Smith, the military commandant. In a reply to a letter sent from Lee, Lieutenant Colonel Smith noted, "My opinion is, that the barracks furnished to the colored troops are as good as the average of those which have been erected for white troops."[111]

Staying warm wasn't the only challenge facing the men at Camp Ward; poor sanitation and inadequate facilities exacted a significant toll on the soldiers of the regiment. In late December, the *Detroit Free Press* reported a tragic incident: a soldier had died on Christmas Eve, allegedly from the effects of poisoning at the camp. Following his death, his body was sent home to his family in Pipestone in Berrien County. An escort, equal in number to that permitted for a captain's interment according to army regulations, accompanied him to the express office, led by the solemn cadence of the regimental band. The circumstances surrounding his death and the somber sendoff underscored the harsh conditions and insufficient care provided to these men, who were left vulnerable to disease and other health risks. This incident revealed the broader issues in camp management and the lack of resources allocated to the welfare of colored soldiers at Camp Ward.[112]

On January 2, 1864, the *Detroit Advertiser & Tribune* reported that the thermometer had reached negative six degrees. This greatly increased the suffering of those quartered at Camp Ward. It was understood to be impossible to stay warm and that nearly every man there had some portion of his body freeze. These conditions became so severe at this time that the commanders decided to order the enlisted men, along with the officers, to leave Camp Ward to find refuge in Detroit, which they then did, scattered around the city. Fortunately, to help with this, the men were issued double blankets. However, the blankets did not account for the low temperature with which they were faced.[113]

Soon after this, officers of the 1st Michigan Colored Regiment adopted the following resolution during a meeting on Saturday, January 2, 1864:

> *We, the undersigned, officers of the 1st Michigan colored regiment, deeply impressed with the importance of providing tenable quarters for our men, earnestly but respectfully protest against the use of the present barracks allotted to us. We are actuated purely by honorable motives, and look only to the comfort of our men. Feeling thus, we have unanimously adopted the following resolutions:*
>
> *Whereas, An investigation having been made by Dr. Charles S. Tripler, U.S.A., by order of Col. Hill, A.A.P.M.G., of this state, and to the condition of the barracks occupied by the 1st Michigan colored regiment, and he having reported that they were untenable for winter and rough weather quarters: be it*
>
> *Resolved, That we earnestly entreat and respectfully request that such improvements be made as well as ensure not only comfort and general health to the men, but render them tenable for the ordinary business necessary to be transacted.*
>
> *Resolved, That, as the report of the medical examiner above named, has explicitly and elaborately stated the precise condition of these quarters, it is unnecessary for us to recapitulate them, but as we beg to testify to the truthfulness of his statement, and vouch for the accuracy thereof.*
>
> *Resolved, That as 50 men are at present suffering from the effect of having been frozen, while in their quarters, and that, too, extra fires were burning, humanity alone suggests that the quarters should be properly fitted up immediately, or the men removed to a rendezvous where they will not undergo sufferings.*
>
> *Resolved, That having seen the publication of a recent letter from Capt. Geo. W. Lee, A Q.M., U.SA. in the Free Press, of this city, referring to these quarters, we cannot but express our disapprobation of his opinions as they're expressed, knowing that they were incorrect, and believing that, if Capt. Lee had made a personal inspection of the buildings, he would have expressed an entirely different opinion.*
>
> *Resolved, That the answer appearing to the publication of the above referred to letter, in the editorial columns of the Advertiser and Tribune,*

subsequently, meets our warmest and hearty approval, being written by one who we have every reason to believe to be well posted upon the unsafe, unhealthy and dilapidated condition of these barracks.

Resolved, That during the construction of the barracks, repeated suggestions were made to Capt. Lee, A.Q.M., U.S.A., in reference to the probable future unfitness of the officers and man's quarters, but notwithstanding these, he ordered them to be constructed according to his own particular notions, disregarding in every particular the claims made upon him for the comfort of the regiment.

Resolved, That a copy of these resolutions will be forwarded to Lieut. Col. J.R. Smith, Military Commandant of the State, with a respectful request that they be forwarded to Major C.W. Foster Chief of the Colored Bureau, at Washington, D.C.; and also the editors of the Advertiser and Tribune and Free Press, of this city, be requested to give them publication.

Capt. D.C. BENJAMIN, President.
Lieut. E.S. JEWETT, Secretary.
E.P. JENNINGS, Assistant Surgeon.
Lieut. IRVING STEVENS, Commanding Co. E.
Lieut. SAMUEL B. CURTIS.
Lieut. JAMES A. MCKNIGHT.
G.A. SOUTHWORTH, Lieut. Com'dg Co A.
P.E. MEAD 2d Lieut Co. B.
Lieut. CHAS. L. BARRELL, Com'dg Co. C.
Lieut. EDWARD DUBENDORFF, Com'dg Co. D.
Lieut. VOLNEY POWERS, Co. G.[114]

The *Detroit Advertiser & Tribune* backed these complaints:

Whoever the shoe may fit, we have no hesitation in saying that the treatment of the Colored regiment in the matter of the barracks has been brutally inhuman. There is not a barn or pigsty in the whole city of Detroit that is not more fit for the habitation of a human-being than the quarters at Camp Ward. They are built of the meanest lumber and in the shabbiest manner, and are not in the slightest degree weatherproof...To send them back to their present barracks is simply to commit murder.[115]

The *Tribune* also described some of the recent daily issues the men were facing before having to abandon the camp:

> *On Thursday night the rain poured through the roof in torrents, and, wetting through triple thicknesses of blanket, froze stiff upon the very bodies of the wretched soldiers. On Friday, notwithstanding enormous fires, the wind rushed in through the gaping cracks in the sides of the miserable shed, and over fifty men were badly frozen, despite the most vigorous efforts to prevent this result.*[116]

A letter was sent to U.S. Quartermaster Lee by Major Foster of the Adjutant General's Bureau in Washington, D.C., instructing him to make such repairs. However, Lee denied ever receiving such a letter. In mid-January 1864, the U.S. Army Quartermaster Department ordered Captain G.W. Lee to make the needed repairs to Camp Ward.[117] However, before the repairs were made, many men became ill, and twenty-five died. In addition, most of the regiment's desertions came during this time. Other men moved into town to stay with friends and relatives. The situation became unbearable for many of the soldiers, leading them to desert the regiment—122 of the 187 total desertions (65 percent) for the 1st Michigan colored Regiment (102nd USCT) were recorded between December 1863 and March 1864.[118]

Chapter 10

Presentation of the Colors

On January 5, 1864, at 2:00 p.m., a large crowd gathered in spite of the weather for a special ceremony at Camp Ward. The regiment was formed into its hollow square formation, enclosing the crowd. John D. Richards presented the 1st Michigan Colored Infantry a regimental flag on behalf of the Colored Ladies Soldiers Aid Society of Detroit.[119]

During the presentation, John D. Richards made these remarks:

> *Officers and soldiers of the 1st Colored Regiment Michigan Volunteers—The Ladies of the Colored Soldiers' Aid Society have requested me to present you this beautiful banner, as an evidence of their admiration of the part you have assumed in stirring scenes of the day. It is a glorious thing to be an American soldier, but thrice glorious when you know that every blow you strike will help you unrivet the chains with which centuries of prejudice have bound us. You have hopes and prayed for the day when, under the good old flag of the Union, you could take up arms in its defense, and prove to the oppressors of our race, that although they have wronged us, still we could forgive—that although they had brutalized us as far as human agencies could accomplish it, we still had sufficient of manhood and love of liberty left to strike, when by striking we could be free—that although you have been degraded to the level of the brute, although your minds have been shrouded in the gloom of the artificial night, yet the idea that you were born to be free has survived it all. As this beautiful banner floats above our heads, my mind wanders to distant fields of strife upon which it shall*

proudly borne aloft, a witness of the bravery and daring of the only race among whom there are no traitors to the Union. Emblazoned on the folds of this banner is an eagle guarding the Stars and Stripes—that sacred emblem of American Liberty—and as I deliver it into your hands, I only hope and trust that you will exercise for it the same sleepless vigilance—the same matchless devotion—the same undying affection.

The contest between freedom and oppression is as old as the world, and has culminated on this continent in the great rebellion now raging in the land. You are called upon for the first time in our history, in common with other men, to play a part in this drama, and to assist in working out upon this continent the destiny of the human family. God seems to be carrying the nation though the fire of purification, that they may exhibit to the world a great free Republic, in which all men are truly free. Take this banner, then, and let ever let it wave in honor above you, and when in the heat of the contest your eye shall see its eagle proudly borne aloft, let it nerve your hearts, and remember that upon you are turned the eyes of the world, and upon you rest the hope of humanity.[120]

Miss Betty Martin then handed the flag to Colonel Henry Barns. Following the flag presentation, the chaplain of the regiment, Mr. William Waring, entered the square and presented Lieutenant Colonel William T. Bennet with a sword, sash and belt on behalf of the noncommissioned officers and privates of the regiment. This sword was of European make with a beautiful pattern and cost about $130. The belt was richly jeweled, with the end being mounted with a large carbuncle, surrounded by rubies. The blade was made of Damascene steel, richly chased, and the scabbard was inscribed with the following: "Presented to Col. Wm. T. Bennett by the Non-commissioned Officers and Privates of the 1st Michigan Colored Regiment."[121]

Chaplain William Waring made these remarks:

Colonel Bennett—The non-commissioned officers and men of your command present to you this sword and belt, as a slight token of the respect which they entertain for you as a man and an officer. If there was nothing more connected with this presentation than the mere intrinsic value of these articles, there would be nothing particularly flattering, either to the donors, or to you as the recipient. But, sir, the unusual circumstances which surround this nation at this time, and which have called into existence not only this command, but many similar ones, lend dignity and character to this occasion. And in the light of these circumstances, this sword and

> *belt are nothing less than an expression of their confidence in your ability as a leader; an evidence of their willingness to trust in your hands their happiness and prosperity as soldiers; and the belief on their part, that the maintenance of their honor will not be neglected.*
>
> *Take, then, this sword, with the warmest wishes of the donors for your personal welfare and safety; and may you wear it with honor, and when these men may see it flash along the line of battle, may the answering fires of liberty within their hearts be kindled anew, and their arms strengthened to strike telling blows for God and humanity.*[122]

Lieutenant Colonel Bennett carefully received the sword into his possession and made these remarks:

> *Officers and men of the Colored Regiment, you have presented me with a testimonial of your esteem, which I shall relinquish only with death. I sincerely thank you for it. Did I prize the gift only for its pecuniary value, I should return it with the request that you present it to your families. But I fancy there is a principle involved in this sword, and I shall keep it as a talisman to the future renown of this regiment. There are many men among you who, before this Administration accorded you the name of freemen, had at the greatest peril risked their lives and limbs, over torturous roads, to reach this Northern ground. You are men who have laughed at danger. You will do it again. Your noble brother soldiers at Port Hudson, at Fort Wagner, defied the rebel threat that no quarter would be shown to you or your officers, by hurling in their teeth a response of shot and steel. When this war is over, the fate of the noble colored men at Milliken's Bend will be told with pride by all those who have borne an honorable part in it. It will then be told how 2,500 colored men—many of whom had never seen or handled a musket until the morning of that memorable attack—with bayonets fixed and clenched teeth, charged wildly through 3000 rebels, and drove them from the field without firing a shot. The sequel of their valor lay upon the field, where not a dead rebel was found whose brains were not dashed out with the butt end of a musket.*
>
> *You have proven that the African has lost nothing of that martial renown which made him the terror of Europe when Hannibal led his hosts across the Alps. You have proven that Southern fetters have failed to crush that invincible spirit which is the chief element of manhood. We who had boasted of our national greatness—who had arrogantly set the example of justice and equality to the world, but who maintained upon*

> *our national escutcheon the foul, damning blot of slavery—are finally compelled to admit that a dark hand can handle a musket as firmly and patriotically as a white one. I had seen much of colored people, not only in this but in foreign countries, where color is no standard of merit or virtue, but I had yet to return to Michigan, the State of my birth, to find myself, as I now do, surrounded by a class of colored men whose patriotism in future ages will be a monument of rebuke to the traitorous factions by whom you are surrounded.*[123]

The men and woman overwhelmingly cheered following Bennett's remarks. Following the cheer, the 624-man regiment formed into line, led by its exceptional brass band, and marched its way down the streets of Detroit, showcasing its new banner with pride. The men's fascinating appearance attracted positive attention throughout the city.[124]

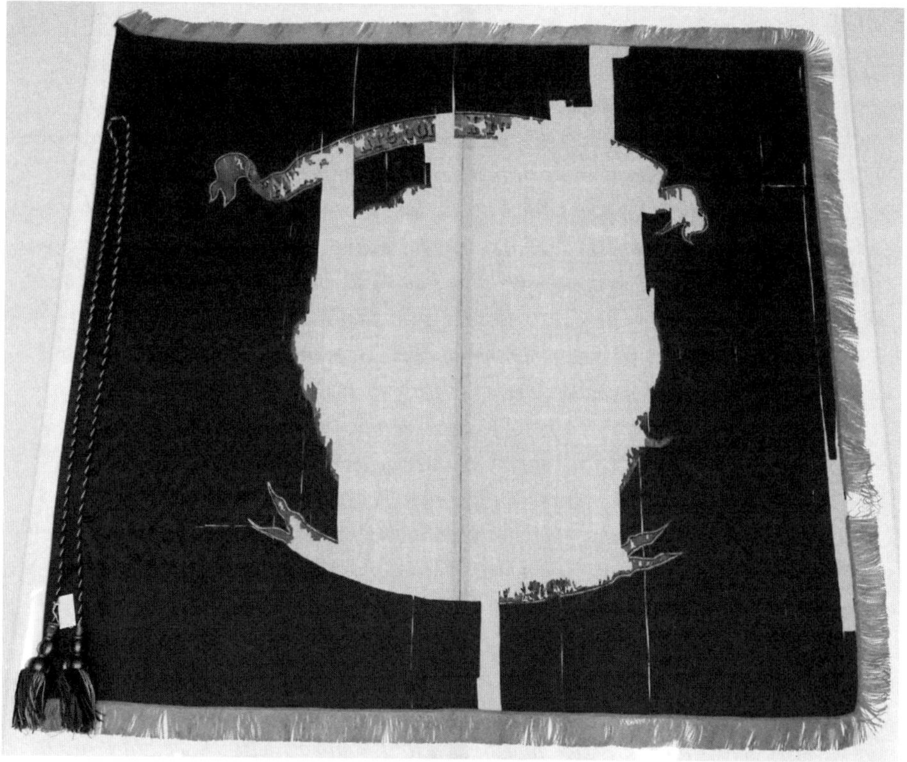

One side of the regiment's presentation flag after conservation. Most of the painted area is missing because the paint made the silk more fragile and susceptible to loss. *Michigan State Capitol.*

The flag presented that day was a regimental flag made by Robert Hopkin of the firm Laible, Wright & Hopkin. This flag was made of blue silk with a yellow fringe around the edge. Attached to the staff were tassels of red, white and blue. One side of the flag featured the state coat of arms, with the words, "Presented by the Colored Ladies' Soldiers' Aid Society of Detroit to the First Colored Regiment Michigan Infantry, 1863" in the scroll work. On the reverse side of the flag was the representation of an eagle guarding the banner of the Union. This side read, "All men are born free and equal, To realize which, we fight." Before being presented to the regiment, the flag was on display at Laible & Co.'s salesrooms on Jefferson Avenue. This flag is now held in the Michigan State Battle Flag Collection.[125]

Chapter 11

Strength in Unity

Where they were able to, female family members worked to support the troops during their time of training in Michigan. This was the goal of the Colored Ladies Soldiers Aid Society of Detroit. Some families even moved to Detroit to stay close. On December 4, 1863, the *Detroit Free Press* reported that around thirty family members of enlisted soldiers of the colored regiment arrived in Detroit from the South a few days prior. The State of Michigan's Volunteer Relief Fund helped families such as these.[126]

On February 11, 1864, the 1st Michigan Colored Regiment was reviewed by Lieutenant Colonel Joseph Rowe Smith, the military commandant, who was joined by a delegation from Windsor, Ontario. This delegation included Captain Armstrong of the Royal Canadian Rifles, Mayor Samuel MacDonnell, Dr. O'Brien and Mr. Higgins. Colonel J.K. Miner and Colonel Henry Barns also joined them in watching the review. Led by Lieutenant Colonel Bennett, the regiment marched to a vacant lot on the northeast corner of Woodward Avenue and High Street near St. John's Episcopal Church. With their brass band leading the march, the men arrived at two o'clock. For nearly two and a half hours, the men drilled and were immaculately put through the most complicated maneuvers of the period.[127]

Following the drill, the men were formed into their hollow square formation, and Colonel J.R. Smith addressed the regiment from inside. Colonel Smith complimented the men on their discipline and efficiency but noted that their first duty of a soldier is to be obedient, avoid the use of "spirituous liquors" and disregard all tendencies to unruly conduct. He further added that colored men had proved themselves to be good and true soldiers and felt convinced that they would not be behind their brethren in the performance of the high trust reposed in them.[128]

At the conclusion of the speech, the regiment performed a few more maneuvers, finishing by forming a square four columns deep—the first column kneeling, the second column at charge bayonet, the third column at arms port and the final column at shoulder arms. The forming of this square was done flawlessly and impressed the large audience in attendance. On the way back to Camp Ward, marching through Woodward and Jefferson Avenues, the regiment formed into a hollow square and impressively held the position correctly during the rest of the march. The *Advertiser & Tribune* reported the following day saying, "They are a fine body of men, and are entitled to all the praise that can be bestowed upon them."[129]

The *Detroit Free Press* astonishingly gave compliments in its report about this occasion, commending their precision in drill and the performance of the brass band. However, to no surprise, its report did not conclude without some sneer remark, adding that "the regiment now claims to be full to the minimum. If such is the case, by all means let it be sent into the field at once, where it can be of some service. Its day of usefulness in Detroit is past, and its place is now in the front, that those massive feet may be put to good use and trampling down this quote 'unholy rebellion.'"[130]

Chapter 12

Returning for Justice

Colored Canadians Join the Fight

During the Civil War, many colored Canadians who had escaped slavery or were the descendants of fugitive slaves returned to the United States to enlist in the Union army. Many of these individuals had initially fled to Canada through the Underground Railroad, a secret network of abolitionists and safe houses that helped enslaved people escape from the United States to freedom in Canada. Although they had found safety in Canada, the prospect of fighting for the liberation of others still enslaved in the South motivated many to take up arms. Among these was Elijah Willis, who left his farm near Chatham, Ontario, and crossed the border to Detroit, hoping to organize a company of Black volunteers. However, since colored men were not permitted to enlist during this early part of the war, such permission to raise a company could not be authorized. Some offered more courteous refusals than others, but the response was always the same.

Now, with Colonel Barns's regiment in the recruiting process, it marked a turning point for many colored Canadians who had sought a way to fight against slavery. For some, it meant crossing the border once again to enlist, returning to a country that had once enslaved them or their ancestors. Many of these soldiers had come from families who had escaped slavery in the Southern United States, and the opportunity to fight for the freedom of their fellow African Americans was a deeply personal mission. The records show that more than one thousand of the 1st Michigan Colored Regiment were born in slave states; many of those born in the South were either fugitive slaves or the sons of fugitive slaves. A good number of soldiers originated from Canadian communities such as Buxton and Chatham, where thousands of fugitive slaves had settled. Despite international law forbidding the recruitment of soldiers in Canada for foreign conflicts, recruitment efforts for Black regiments were conducted surreptitiously. Many African Canadians crossed the Detroit River at Windsor to enlist in the Union army. Some of these men were former slaves who had taken leadership roles within their communities, helping others navigate the journey back to the United States for enlistment. These individuals not only fought for the Union but also played a critical role in guiding their fellow Black Canadians to enlist in the fight against the Confederacy.[131]

Among the community of former slaves, there were individuals with a natural talent for leadership who dedicated themselves to guiding others on the path to enlistment. These leaders, driven by the hope of freedom and empowerment for their people, spent considerable time helping fellow Black individuals reach Detroit or nearby states to join the ranks. One notable figure was Mrs. Shad-Cary, a former enslaved woman whose maiden name was Shad before she married Thomas Cary. She split her efforts between Detroit and Chatham, and among Detroit's older Black families, her memory remains cherished with deep respect. Mrs. Shad-Cary personally escorted dozens of former slaves from Canada, guiding them to the enlistment location and inspiring others along the way. Her work was echoed by other committed leaders in or around Chatham, such as David Williamson, George Sorell, a blacksmith known as Mr. Street and Elijah Willis, all of whom tirelessly worked to support this cause.[132]

Lorenzo Rann, a twenty-two-year-old Canadian born resident of the Buxton settlement in Ontario, was one such individual who went to the United States to fight in the 1st Michigan Colored Regiment. Rann, like many others, believed in the importance of fighting to end slavery, despite already being a lifelong freeman himself. His service in the United States came at a personal cost, as during a battle in South Carolina, he sustained a serious injury to his leg when a shell exploded near him. This injury would take him out of action, being discharged for disability, and affect him for the rest of his life. But Rann's commitment to the cause of freedom never wavered. After the war, he struggled with poor health and financial difficulties, eventually applying for admission to the Michigan Soldiers' Home in Grand Rapids, where he lived until his death in 1922.[133]

The participation of Black Canadians like Lorenzo Rann and many others in the 1st Michigan Colored Regiment underscores the transnational nature of the fight for freedom. Although they had found safety and security in Canada, many African Canadians felt a deep sense of obligation to help end slavery in the United States. Their return to the battlefields of the South as soldiers in the 1st Michigan Colored Regiment and other Union units was not only a courageous act of self-sacrifice but also a powerful statement about their commitment to the fight for justice and equality. Their contributions helped shape the course of the war and the ultimate abolition of slavery in the United States.[134]

Chapter 13

Trouble at Camp Ward

Although the regiment had been presented with its flag, they remained in Detroit for several more months before being deployed to the battlefield. During this period, local newspapers continued to comment on the regiment's condition and the suitability of its men. Detroit's two major newspapers, with differing political affiliations, offered contrasting perspectives in their coverage. In February and March, the *Detroit Free Press* and the *Detroit Advertiser & Tribune* reported on two separate incidents involving a small group of men from the 1st Michigan Colored Regiment engaging in saloon brawls.[135]

On February 21, 1864, the *Detroit Advertiser & Tribune* reported that several men of the regiment had "become quite noisy" at a local saloon; it was believed that a fight was imminent. Lieutenant Edward Cahill, overhearing the noise, came to the saloon to calm the situation.[136]

Corporal John Thompson, overseeing the other enlisted men at the saloon, disregarded all attempts by Lieutenant Cahill to interfere, allegedly even going so far as to order the men to fire on their officer. However, this was thankfully prevented, and the men returned to Camp Ward right after. The men causing the disturbance were disciplined by their officers and placed in the guard house upon return. The paper made sure to mention, "The regiment as a general thing, is composed of good fighting material, are very peaceable, and if there be any among them that are not willing to learn military discipline, they should, for the good of the organization, be

Edward Cahill (1843–1922) joined the Union Army auring the Civil War, initially serving in Kentucky and later raising Michigan's first African American infantry unit, eventually attaining the rank of captain. After the war, he pursued a legal career and was appointed to the Michigan Supreme Court in 1890 to replace Justice Thomas R. Sherwood. Although he lost his subsequent election, Cahill's contributions to Michigan's legal community were significant, and he remained a respected figure throughout his career. *Michigan Supreme Court Historical Society.*

taught it in a summary manner." By contrast, *Detroit Free Press* graphically described all the injuries sustained by white patrons resulting from the barroom fight. The paper used derogatory language to refer to the men of the regiment and painted the men as a thieving mob. This article showed some of the racism the men of the regiment faced, even while serving in uniform in a Northern state.[137]

Corporal Thompson was court-martialed for several serious offenses related to his conduct on February 19, 1864. The court found Thompson guilty on multiple charges, and his sentence was severe. He was reduced in rank, had his chevrons stripped in front of his regiment and forfeited all pay and future bounties. Thompson was also sentenced to imprisonment with hard labor at Fort Clinch, Florida, and was to be drummed out of service upon completion of his sentence. Although a procedural issue was noted regarding his plea to one of the charges, the verdict stood, with the court including the phrase "said Corporal and soldiers with him all having loaded guns." Major General Heintzelman ultimately approved the sentence, ordering it to be executed under the supervision of Thompson's regiment.[138]

In a letter from Fort Marion, St. Augustine, Florida, dated May 4, 1865, Thompson appealed to Major General Gilmore, claiming that he was wronged in his case. He explained that he had followed previous orders to patrol Detroit but was unfairly accused of mutiny and insubordination. Thompson described being forcibly arrested and tried without proper representation. He pleaded for his release and a chance to rejoin his regiment, vowing to be a loyal and obedient soldier if given the opportunity. Thompson's letter reflects his sense of injustice and his hope that higher authorities would intervene on his behalf.[139]

About one week after the saloon incident, another conflict in Detroit occurred when two white soldiers and one soldier of the colored regiment got into a heated argument on the corner of Larned and Griswold Streets. One of the white soldiers punched the colored soldier and stormed off. The colored soldier then turned around and punched the remaining white soldier. The other white soldier came back to rejoin the brawl, and the colored soldier pulled a revolver out and struck a serious blow, knocking one white soldier to the ground. Now in a panic, the colored soldier fled down Griswold Street toward Jefferson Avenue with a large crowd yelling "Stop him!" Arriving at the street corner, the colored soldier used some bystanders for his protection. Now with a large crowd assembled, a street fight began to broil when Officer William H. broke his way through into the onlookers, securing the revolver and putting an end to the rowdy affair.[140]

With the situation on Larned and Griswold Streets quelled, another heated conflict was brewing on Croghan Street in a place called Buckner's. Sheriff's deputies were attempting to take a white woman into custody when several colored soldiers and others came to her defense with their bayonets and revolvers drawn. Under this pressure, the deputies released the woman. Several of the soldiers then made their way back to Camp Ward, with the sheriff's deputies following, intending to arrest them. Upon arrival, the deputies came into contact with Colonel Henry Barns, who gave them permission to enter the camp and continue with their mission. The colored soldiers intervened in the discussion and, after a quick debate, started after one of the deputies but were blocked by Colonel Barns. Following this altercation, the deputies decided not to pursue the matter further and made their way back into the city.[141]

While most issues reported by local newspapers took place outside Camp Ward, one soldier found himself bringing attention to issues inside of the camp. On the afternoon of Friday, February 19, 1864, one soldier, in a playful mood, aimed his musket and pulled the trigger. Unfortunately, the rifle was loaded. With a *crack* the ball struck a young nineteen-year-old soldier, Benjamin Green, in the back of his neck, passing through his spine and out the other side of his body. The ball continued, striking another soldier in the shoulder and passing entirely through him. The first soldier was in critical condition, lying paralyzed. Unfortunately, the young soldier would die just a few days later on February 21. For the soldier who fired the shot, he was immediately arrested and placed in the guardhouse at Camp Ward.[142]

Less than a month later, on the night of Wednesday, March 23, it was reported by the *Detroit Free Press* that several colored soldiers broke into the residence/store of John Burger, who lived nearby Camp Ward on Macomb Street. It was said that the soldiers made their way through a rear window of the structure and began to take clothing and two decanters. The men left through the front door, which made a noise, waking Mr. Burger, who then looked out his upstairs bedroom window and saw the colored soldiers running down the street with the stolen items.[143]

Dr. Curtis, who was with some company commanders at the time they were informed of the innocent, had this to say about the matter the following morning: "There came a messenger, stating that some of our boys were cleaning out a whiskey shop. It was not long before we were on the ground and found that a German saloon keeper had been cleaned out, and two Dutchmans were cut up pretty bad, but not enough to hurt them much! Well, the truth of the matter is this: they gave the soldiers whiskey, and they got used up. By the means, there is great excitement in town on the account of it. The report says that the old man was badly hurt, but that is not so, for I saw the wounded and dressed the wound on the old man's head and the other. I am sure he will not!"[144]

Prior to the incident at Mr. Burger's residence, another barroom fight occurred on March 18 reported by the *Detroit Free Press*. According to the paper, a clash broke out at a saloon on the corner of Croghan and Russell Streets, where a group of colored soldiers allegedly assaulted a white civilian named Nicholas Kale following a dispute during a billiards game. The soldiers reportedly returned with reinforcements, attacked Kale and fired shots in the street with revolvers. Order was restored only after a white officer arrived with troops to march the men back to their barracks, and the mayor vowed to pursue arrests. Unfortunately, this was only the start for what would be a rough week for the regiment. It would only be a week later, on Thursday, March 24, 1864, that soldiers of the regiment would find themselves in more trouble. During that evening, around twenty colored soldiers, excited for liquor and cigars, entered Mr. John Hollstein's saloon on the corner of Lafayette and Rivard Streets. The *Detroit Free Press* described the instance as follows:

> *Hollstein being in the saloon at the time, went behind the bar, and handed out a decanter containing whiskey, several glasses, and a box of cigars. One of the darkies nearest the counter, then caught hold of the box, and put it under his arm. Hollstein took hold of him by the arm and requested him to lay the box back upon the counter. The negro refused to comply with his demand, and turned about as if to leave the saloon, when Hollstein started to shut the door which had been left open. He had got about halfway across the room when one of the negroes took one of the glasses from the counter and threw it at him, striking him just over the eye, slivering the tumbler and inflicting three deep gashes, one of them about an inch in depth, together with several smaller cuts, and causing him to stagger back against the wall. Bleeding profusely, he then turned about, ran upstairs, and, grasping a double-barrel shot-gun, which was in his sleeping room, started with it to return to the saloon, when his wife urged him not to take the weapon down with him, as the negroes would kill him if he did. He then went down stairs into a room adjoining the saloon, where he washed and bandaged up his wounds, and went in search of officer Gnau.*
>
> *Meanwhile the negroes had begun to look for a second victim, which they found in the person of an old man of seventy, Francis Rohnert, who was seated near the stove, a quiet spectator of the scene. A stalwart negro, snatching a large earthen water pitcher from the counter, dealt the aged man a heavy blow over the eye, which made a deep wound, driving one rim of his spectacles into the gash, and stretching him senseless upon the floor. They then turned down the gas and commenced their work of plunder. They robbed the saloon of all its cigars, drained the money drawer of its contents, took the decanters from the shelves, drank the liquor they contained, and then dashed them to pieces on the floor. After completely gutting the saloon they broke in the windows, and then sallied forth in quest of new adventures.*[145]

Following this matter, six troops of that group split off and went to Henry Schoeppe's saloon nearby on the corner of Croghan and Rivard Streets. After having some whiskey, the rest was scattered on the saloon's floor. Schoeppe, now seeing where the evening would be heading, went into the back and came out with a loaded rifle that was also equipped with his bayonet. Local Justice Kuhn entered the saloon as this was happening and demanded that both groups withdraw from the matter. Other soldiers of the main group went to the saloon of P. Drexelius on the corner of Macomb and Russell Streets. Finding the saloon locked, it was reported that the soldiers broke the front windows.[146]

This was the final straw for Colonel Barns. The following day, he issued orders not to grant passes to soldiers of the regiment after 4:00 p.m. Barns further added that any soldier found absent from the camp later than this hour would be liable to arrest for desertion. Barns felt that this new order would stop all unlawful proceedings pertaining to his regiment.[147]

However, not long after, another incident occurred on March 26, 1864, when the soldiers made a rally on the "sutler's shanty"; as Captain Nelson described, they "tore it up pretty bad before I got out to them." The next day, on March 27, 1864, a more critical incident occurred when a drunk soldier of Company K caused a "disturbance" in one of the barracks. The soldier was arrested by the orderly sergeant. However, while being escorted to the guardhouse, the private became violent and pulled out a knife. In the tussle, the private managed to stab and inflict an almost fatal wound on the orderly sergeant. Fortunately the orderly sergeant was able to recover from his wounds at a nearby home on Woodbridge Street. For the private, it was found that he had past conduct issues, having been guilty of other crimes and misdemeanors before. A court-martial headed by the drum took place immediately, and the disorderly private was sentenced to death by firing squad. The sentence was to be carried out upon arrival at Annapolis, Maryland.[148]

While the soldiers would sometime find themselves in mischief, that did not change the perspective of their white comrades in the regiment. Such was the case when Corporal Thomas Tennett of the regiment found himself in trouble. In December 1864, Corporal Tennett was arrested for battery on a police officer and was fined ten dollars—if in default of payment, he would serve twenty-five days in the House of Correction. Unfortunately, Corporal Tennett did not have funds to pay for the fine. However, he pleaded to the policemen that he could get the funds back at the barracks. The police officers then escorted the detained the soldier down to Camp Ward, where he was taken into process by a military officer of the regiment. Through some conversation, Corporal Tennett had his fine paid for in full by the sutler of regiment. This act of kindness by the white sutler certainly helps us to understand the relationship between the colored soldiers and their white counterparts.[149]

The *Detroit Free Press* continuously sought out flaws to publish on the colored regiment but would often create its own opinions when no such flaws could be found within a reasonable time. The *Free Press* would go so far to dehumanize the men of this regiment in publishing an article titled "Raid of the First Ethiopians." The *Advertiser & Tribune* accused the *Free*

Press of trying to arouse the hatred of the community against the regiment with its biased and inaccurate reporting:[150]

Raid of the First Ethiopians

We have often wondered why Barns' Ethiopian Troops were quartered on a bleak upland, in the city, during this inclement weather, while, under the lead of their gallant Colonel, they might be distinguishing and extinguishing themselves in their native Sunny South. This is one of the unaccountable things of the times, but is certainly no fault of the Colonel. The government may prefer to keep them here to die with the smallpox rather than send them South to pour out their life blood in the "sacred cause of human freedom," but the Colonel seems determined that their time shall not be altogether wasted. Every precious moment is spent in drilling men and fitting them for the field, and in cultivating in them a warlike and belligerent spirit.

He is practicing them in every maneuver, thanking them, digging trenches (for the benefit of the smallpox patients), and Saturday night he led them forth on an extensive raid. At the dead hour of night, when everybody was supposed to be in bed, the regiment silently and cautiously set out from their camp. The sight was an inspiring one. At the head of the column rode the gallant Colonel, mounted on the noble war-horse recently presented to him by his admiring friends, and which was for some time on exhibition to the public on the Campus Martius. Next to him, chief of his staff, rode the famous African known about town as "King Cotton," anxiously inquiring if his Wayne county bounty is to be paid in shingle bales. The whole regiment was in line soon after twelve o'clock, and "not a drum was heard" as they moved past the nearest henroost.

The "band" had been, after some effort, relentlessly choked off from performing their favorite tune on this occasion. As the sable heroes moved along, the whites of their eyes and their teeth glistened in the starlight, so completely outshining the bayonets that the latter made no effort, knowing they could not do themselves credit. Silently the regiment moved through the back streets, and before the solitary policeman, who guards the upper part of the town, was aware of their presence, they were in the heart of the city. On the Campus Martius they drew up in line of battle, and, without firing a gun, charged upon and captured the sable African who has, for some years past, had charge of a pestle and mortar on the top of a high post in front of the Russell House. This was one of the most successful raids of the war. The capture was made without the slightest resistance on the part of the prisoner, and without firing a gun, although the regiment was supplied with ten rounds of cartridges and four hours rations.

Having accomplished the object of their reconnaissance, the regiment retired to their quarters and slept until after breakfast. We shall watch with some interest for the Colonel's official report of this affair, as it is certain that all distinguished themselves, and there will be universal promotion. Col. Barns has already earned the star, and the filling out of the necessary blanks is now all that is required to make him a Brigadier.[151]

Another example of false reporting on the colored regiment would come on March 3, 1864, when the band of the 1st Michigan held a dance at the local Merrill Hall on Woodward Avenue. The following article was published in a local paper the next day:

Grand Artillery Shake Down—The Colored Citizens and Soldiers Indulged in a "Hep."

Last evening was what "A. Ward" would term "an episode" in the lives of the colored brethren and slaters of Detroit and Camp Ward. They gathered in their strength, and until & clock this morning, shook the light fantastic heel, to their own delight and that of several "poor white trash" present to witness the performance. Merrill Hall was the scene of these festivities, and as such will "rank" among the first halls of the city, until long after the present generation cease to snuff the air of heaven. Upwards of a hundred couple participated in the amusements, and verified the old maxim that "in Union there is strength."

Among the ladies present were many of the colored aristocracy of the city, whose beauty, and the ease with which they supported the dignity devolving upon them as belles of the occasion, illustrates in a high degree the natural talents of the race. There were many of the opposite sex evidently enamored of their partners, and the languishing looks cast by them upon the fair features of their love, was only prevented from bringing to the check the tell-tale blush on account of the presence of too much color.

This revelry was kept up with undiminished interest until in the "small hours," when began the somewhat difficult task of separating the followers of the meek and lowly Barns from the cautious darkies—the soldier from the civilian—at which time it was discovered that a very fair proportion had become fatigued by repeated attacks upon the defenses around neighboring saloons, and surrendered themselves willing captives. What was the object of this ball, whether simply to give the soldiers a little harmless recreation,

> *or a benefit to Col. Barns, to render a little assistance, in repaying the large sums lost by him in his philanthropic efforts to improve their condition, was not stated in the bill, but the latter is the generally conceded purpose. If so, the gallant Colonel certainly fell short of what might be expected of him in not gracing the festivities by his presence.*[152]

The *Detroit Advertiser & Tribune* would go on to address the variety of altercations taking place in the city pertaining to the 1st Michigan Colored Regiment. The paper would first call out the lies and false "outrages" put forward by the *Detroit Free Press* about members of the colored regiment. Relating the incidents of the current time to the riots of 1863, the *Tribune* further added that it had been about one year since the "persistent falsehoods of this organ culminated in a bloody and destructive riot." It was said in a few incidents that the unruly member of the colored regiment may have distributed public order; however, their orderlies have persistently and efficiently punished such behavior.[153]

Continuing to push back against the critics, rumors and slander, the *Detroit Advertiser & Tribune* said that "in fact, considering the constant abuse showered upon peaceable members of the regiment by 'roughs' and 'semi-rebels,' we wonder that the disturbances have not been of a more sanguinary nature and of more frequent occurrence. Considering the provocation given, we hold that the regiment have displayed more patience and love of law, than could have been expected from ordinary human nature." While some members of the colored regiment did give in to negative provocation at times, the behavior of those individuals was not condoned or endorsed by the regiment as a body.[154]

In a final dismissal, the *Detroit Advertiser & Tribune* stated, "We do not believe that any regiment has ever been encamped in our city for an equal length of time, whose general bearing and conduct have been any less prejudicial to the welfare of our city and the safety of our citizens. We have yet to hear of any well-confirmed case of unprovoked Vandalism on their part. The lies of the *Free Press* deserve sharp public condemnation, and will receive it at the hands of every law-loving and loyal citizen."[155]

It is important to note that according to historical records, the number of incidents, including courts-martial and arrests, of the 1st Michigan Colored Regiment was identical to those of other regiments during the war. Through studies of the behavior of soldiers from other regiments, one sees similarities and commonalities in soldiers' drunk and disorderly behavior across the country.[156]

Chapter 14

From Trouble to Triumph

The boys who enlisted from the Michigan Boys' Reform School into the 1st Michigan Colored Regiment came from a reformatory that had just opened its doors five years before the Civil War began. Initially founded as a place to correct juvenile offenders without sending them to adult prisons, the school quickly found itself burdened by the strains of the war. As the conflict intensified, Superintendent Cephas Robinson faced overcrowding, financial shortfalls and understaffing, yet he saw the war as an opportunity. Many of the boys, including those who had disciplinary issues, were granted "conditional tickets of leave," allowing them to enlist in the Union army as a way of alleviating the school's population and budgetary woes.[157]

Opened in 1856, the reform school aimed to provide rehabilitation to young boys caught in the justice system. However, by the time the Civil War erupted, the school was facing significant challenges, including a swelling population, inadequate funds and the departure of staff members to join the war effort. With nearly all state resources diverted toward the war, Robinson's ability to maintain the institution was severely constrained, and his financial situation became increasingly dire. Desperate for solutions, Robinson saw the war as a potential outlet for some of the older boys, particularly those who were difficult to manage or had no parental oversight.[158]

The 1st Michigan Colored Regiment drew several of these young enlistees, including four eighteen-year-olds: Charles Crockett, Charles Points, George Morgan and Benjamin Green, who was accidentally fatally shot at Camp Ward. At nineteen years old, Benjamin Brooks and William Harrison also

In 1860, juvenile offenders at the Lansing reform school were housed in cell blocks, as shown in this photograph. Despite the school's goal of rehabilitation, the prison-like environment reflects the early approaches to juvenile correction. *Capital Area District Library.*

enlisted, bringing the total enlistees from the Michigan Boys' Reform School in this regiment to six.[159]

For many of the boys who enlisted in Michigan regiments, the decision was driven by a mix of patriotism, financial incentives and, for some, the hope of escaping the restrictions of the reformatory. The $100 enlistment bounty, a significant sum at the time, was a strong lure, especially for boys from impoverished backgrounds. Some families even saw their sons' enlistment as a way to gain much-needed financial relief, often keeping the majority of the bounty for themselves.[160]

Despite their youth and troubled pasts, many of these boys served with distinction. Their letters to the reform school revealed the harsh realities of war, including hunger, disease and the constant threat of death. Yet these letters also showed that the reform school had provided them with a sense of stability and structure. Some boys wrote back to Robinson and the staff as if they were writing home, sharing updates about their experiences in battle and their gratitude for the discipline they had learned at the school. Many proved themselves to be brave and capable soldiers, with some even taking part in key battles like Antietam and Vicksburg.[161]

Although the Civil War placed immense strain on the Michigan Boys' Reform School, it also highlighted the resilience and potential for reform among its charges. These boys, many of whom had once been considered "embryo-criminals," went on to fight valiantly for the Union cause, with some losing their lives in service. For Robinson and the reform school staff, the war served as a testament to the fact that even troubled youth could be rehabilitated and become productive members of society, whether on the battlefield or in civilian life.[162]

Chapter 15

The Refused Escort

Despite their position as soldiers in the army, the young men of the 1st Michigan Colored Regiment's would learn, even before leaving Michigan, that this would not stop distrust from civilians as well as other regiments composed of white men. The renowned band of the colored regiment was in demand in the city of Detroit. Using their talents, the musicians would play at a variety of functions in the city, one of which was to perform in parade fashion during cerebrations of regiments returning from the war front. On March 11, 1864, the men of the 10th Michigan Veteran Infantry Regiment returned home, arriving in Detroit. The regiment, comprising white soldiers, vehemently refused to march up from the depot in the rear of the colored band. The overseeing committee, which employed the band to play for these occasions, was confused by this. This action by the 10th Michigan quickly caused a rift in the city's press on the circumstances.[163]

The *Detroit Free Press*, published the following the day, started by applauding and recognizing the valiant men of 10th Michigan Infantry. The article then added that the honorable men "do not exactly fancy the idea of being escorted to their homes by an African band. The music by some other band would be quite as sweet. We trust that in future, committees of reception will bear this fact in mind. If we cannot give our brave boys such a welcome home and reception as is gratifying and acceptable to them, better give them none at all."[164]

On the other side of the local press, the *Detroit Advertiser & Tribune* wasted no time commenting on the matter, publishing the same day of the incident in its evening edition of the paper. The *Tribune* stated that this was not the first time a matter such as this occurred, but it certainly went farther this time. Prior to this, when the 1st Michigan Infantry Regiment (white) arrived back to the state, there were some unenthusiastic feelings among the men of that regiment. It was said this was because the band of the colored regiment was set forth to parade them through Detroit. Regarding the current matter, it went farther, as all of the companies of the 10th Michigan, with the exception of one, refused to march behind the colored band. The paper called on the committee that arranges the occasion to give a formal explanation on the matter:

> [U]*p to the time the 1st arrived, the Light Guard or City Band has been engaged to discourse music, but their charges—$30 for turning out were considered exorbitant, and as the colored band was the only one remaining that could furnish as good, if not better music, they were requested, and patriotically volunteered their services for a nominal sum. The committee were of the opinion that the other bands, while engaged in escorting veteran soldiers from the depots, should manifest a little spirit of patriotism. They were willing to pay them for their services, but they looked upon their demands for the above amount for such purposes in the light of extortion.*[165]

Later in May 1864, in a letter home, Dr. Curtis shared his opinion of the 10th Michigan, in which some of his friends had enlisted:

> *You say Sim Thomas & his Father was with him. You need not feel bad at what they say for they are confounded fools & traitors. One thing Thank God I am not a member of a drunken rabble like 10th Mich Infty. They are a Regiment of the most God forsaken pups on Gods footstool*[.] *They talk of Niggers. Tell them that a white soldiers here stands equal with the colored men, the whites are not ashamed of fighting by the side of the colored soldiers! As for getting kild that is all in their eye for they take them prisoners down here &c. the record of the 10th Mich is not very bright and they better not brag, for that Animal is a good dog, but Hold em fast is better!*[166]

Continuing to push forward amid the indignities they faced, the fine band of the 1st Michigan Colored Regiment continued to be requested to perform at a variety of gatherings around Detroit, even at several well-attended promenade concerts they sponsored. They also hosted several promenade concerts that were well attended. In the following days, Michigan Governor Austin Blair reviewed the regiment once more on March 15, 1864. The men drilled well and were highly complimented by the governor. Due to the bad weather that day, Governor Blair didn't address the men. However, the men were able to go on parade, headed by their splendid band. Word had also come in that day that the regiment had been assigned to General Burnside's new corps and would report to him in Annapolis, Maryland.[167]

It's a common misconception that numerous women fought openly in the ranks during the Civil War—in fact, documented cases are relatively rare. While a few women did disguise themselves as men to enlist, historical evidence shows that these instances were uncommon, and no records confirm any women serving within the 1st Michigan Colored Regiment. Studies such as *They Fought Like Demons: Women Soldiers in the American Civil War* by DeAnne Blanton and Lauren M. Cook identify only a small number of verified cases, underscoring that women combatants were exceptional rather than typical.[168]

The regiment was officially mustered into federal service by army officer Captain Duryea on Saturday, March 19, 1864. An article in the *Detroit Advertiser & Tribune* mentioned that many of the men had been mustered in previously, but that "this time the whole regiment was sworn in."[169] On the evening of the March 24, 1864, while the men prepared for their departure from the Wolverine State, the Colored Ladies Soldiers Aid Society of Detroit hosted a jamboree and gave a very polite invitation to the white officers. Lieutenant Orson W. Bennett, Second Lieutenant Peter E. Mead and Dr. Curtis took about one hundred men of the colored regiment and marched them down to the hall, where they were dispersed to get their ladies.[170]

Days later, the time had finally come for the men of the 1st Michigan Colored Regiment to head off to war. On March 28, 1864, the regiment was assembled in dress parade, and the orders for the regiment to leave for Annapolis, Maryland, were read aloud. The men were thrilled with the news, waving their caps and cheering. Despite the rainy and snowy weather, the men of the regiment were brought to formation then made their way out of Camp Ward for the last time. Marching down Jefferson Avenue to the Michigan Southern Railroad depot, the regiment came to a stop to give relatives and friends an opportunity to say goodbye to the brave boys. The train left the city of Detroit at noon.

The number of troops aboard the locomotive was debated in the local papers. The *Detroit Advertiser & Tribune* reported that approximately 1,000

1st Michigan Colored Infantry by Stewart Ashlee. *Laura Ashlee.*

soldiers were enlisted in the regiment at this time. However, the *Detroit Free Press* published an article a few days later arguing against this number, stating that Colonel Barns requisitioned transportation to the U.S. quartermaster for between 810 and 850 soldiers. The *Free Press* further added that it attempted to count them while they were aboard the train, counting about 600 soldiers. Pushing an attack on Barns, the *Free Press* said that "charges should be preferred against the Colonel for fraudulently procuring so much transportation than was needed." Michigan records note that the regiment was mustered into service of the United States with 895 men fit for duty on February 17 of that year.[171]

Per the *Detroit Advertiser & Tribune*, the officers and staff of the regiment when leaving Detroit were as follows:

Staff
Colonel—Henry Barns
Lieutenant Colonel—William T. Bennett
Major—Newcomb Clark
Surgeon—Wesley Vincent

Assistant Surgeon—Edward Jennings
Adjutant—James McKnight
Quartermaster—Patrick McLaughlin
Chaplain—William Waring

COMPANY A
First Lieutenant—Orson W. Bennett
Second Lieutenant George Southworth

COMPANY B
Captain—J.P. Benjamin
First Lieutenant—G. Benjamin
Secant Lieutenant—Peter E. Mead

COMPANY C
Captain—Johnathan B. Tuttle
Secant Lieutenant—Charles Barrell

COMPANY D
Captain—Arad E. Lindsay
First Lieutenant—Gilman T. Holmes
Secant Lieutenant—Edward Dubendorff

COMPANY E
Captain—J. McKindry

COMPANY F
Captain—S.B. Bradley
First Lieutenant—Samuel B. Curtis
Secant Lieutenant—Caleb Griffith

COMPANY G
First Lieutenant—Edward Jewett
Secant Lieutenant—James Gilbert

COMPANY H
First Lieutenant—Edmory D. Bryant
Secant Lieutenant—Volney Powors

COMPANY I
First Lieutenant—Wilbur Nelson
Secant Lieutenant—A. VanDyke

COMPANY K
Captain—C.W. Montague
First Lieutenant—Edward Cahill
Secant Lieutenant—George Stoneburn[172]

Chapter 16

Forward for Freedom's Cause

Following the regiment's departure from Detroit, Camp Ward was engulfed in flames. It was reported that the fire was discovered at noon, the same time the regiment departed on the railroad. The fire alarm was sounded, and the local steamers made their way to the former home of the colored regiment. Unfortunately, by their arrival, the fire had become too strong, razing five of the structures to ashes. The *Detroit Free Press* claimed that the colored men had threatened that they would burn down their quarters at Camp Ward before they left; because of this, white soldiers were stationed at the barracks to prevent such. However, this claim was never verified. Several days later, on April 1, the Detroit fire marshal's report in the paper stated, "Five buildings of the barracks burned up. Loss $1,500. Caused by incendiarism on the part of some of colored troops who had that morning been ordered away." The exact cause of the fire remains unknown today.[173]

The 1st Michigan Colored Regiment traveled first to Toledo, where it was to change trains. Upon reaching Toledo, it found that the "Copperhead" post quartermaster, Lee, failed to arrange the necessary transport, and it would take several hours until new train cars would arrive from Cleveland. While the regiment waited, the men made an appearance, forming into a line and marching down Summit Street to Cherry Street. There the regiment held dress parade for the citizens of Toledo. An article from the *Toledo Blade*, reprinted in the *Detroit Advertiser & Tribune*, described the reaction of the crowd: "A large part of our citizens were at the parade, and all appeared pleased with the proficiency of the men in the school of the soldier. With a few exceptions the men demeaned themselves in a very credible manner, showing that their drill-master, Lieut. Col. Bennett, had applied himself diligently to the work of preparing the regiment for usefulness in the field."[174]

After the dress parade, they returned to the depot. The northern area of the depot was given to them to rest until the train was made up. They seated themselves on the floor for the remaining hours and stowed away their rations. After the new train arrived, the 1st Michigan Colored Infantry began its journey toward the front, leaving Toledo at 3:00 a.m. During this brief starting period of their travels, word had gotten around through the papers that Lieutenant Colonel William T. Bennett was expected to be promoted to colonel. Other officers supported this potential promotion, with the *Tribune* noting that these officers were "loud in their praises of his gallantry." The *Toledo Blade* had this to say:[175]

> *Col. Barns is not a military man, and accepted a commission to organize the regiment for the season that he was satisfied colored men were willing and felt it a duty to bear a part in the conflict which was to result in disenthralling millions of their brethren or in reducing themselves to bondage. The Colonel, having completed his task, will return to his post as senior editor of the Detroit Advertiser and Tribune.*[176]

The *Detroit Advertiser & Tribune* quickly responded to the *Toledo Blade*'s article to correct what it felt was false information. The *Tribune* noted that Colonel Barns had not been involved in the *Advertiser & Tribune* for quite some time and that he would not be returning to his previous position of senior editor at the paper. He had retired from the paper to pursue an entirely different line of work. In response to the circulation of these rumors, Barns published a lengthy statement in the *Detroit Advertiser & Tribune*. In this statement, Barns described his two motives to raise the regiment:

> *First, to give the Colored people of this section an opportunity to vindicate their patriotism and bravery, and, second, by such an organization to avoid a draft in this City, County, and State. In the first, I am confident of success—for no regiment except, the "24th Michigan," ever started in Detroit, has progressed as rapidly as the "First Michigan Colored Regiment." In the second I should have succeeded even more satisfactory, and enlisted men sufficient to have entirely avoided a draft in this city and county, but for the persistent opposition of the Free Press, and its constant efforts to bolster up*

> *the humbling pretenders of a so-called "Rhode Island" regiment, in which I take pleasure in saying, the authorities of Rhode Island had no hand. The effect was especially has not a few had been greatly deceived in the "promises" of some engaged in the organization of the "Massachusetts 54th" to create distrust among the colored people, and disheartened and divide the generous interest they had felt for the organization of a regiment of their own race.*[177]

Continuing the journey to Annapolis, Maryland, the 1st Michigan Colored Regiment arrived in Cleveland, Ohio, on March 29, 1864, at 11:00 a.m.[178] The regiment was in good spirits, and each of the men was served a pleasing hot cup of coffee at Mr. Wheeler's dining hall after arriving in the city. The regiment continued, reaching Dunkirk, New York, by midnight, where it once again changed railcars. The men reached Elmira, New York, about noon. Here the men of the regiment drew rations and exchanged cars for the last time en route to Baltimore, Maryland, aboard the Pennsylvania Central Railroad. The regiment was placed into two trains with about one hundred white soldiers aboard as well. The trains were made up of boxcars, cattle cars and one passenger coach for the officers, which "stood no sight for cleanliness by the side of a hog pen," according to Dr. Curtis.[179]

The regiment reached Williamsport, Pennsylvania, at about 5:00 a.m., making seventy-five miles in twelve hours, but not without issue. During that night and the early hours of the day, the regiment faced heavy snowstorms, with the accumulation reaching about a foot deep, contributing to the train running off the track twice. The two trains were made into one, after which they proceeded down the Susquehanna Valley, with "the river on one side of track and the rocks rising hundreds of feet on the other side of us presenting a grand appearance." With everything continuing on schedule, the regiment passed through Harrisburg, Pennsylvania, during the late evening and reached Baltimore, Maryland, the following morning during sunrise on April 1, 1864.[180]

Their travels through Pennsylvania and New York were rough not only due to heavy snow but also due to negative public interactions along the way. The Pennsylvanians were said to have "manifested that same mean, mercenary spirit which led them last summer to charge our soldiers for lint and bandages after the battle of Gettysburg." A reporter traveling with the regiment further added, "There seems to be a systematic arrangement on part of the conductors and employees of the railroad to misuse us, and in every possible manner prevent us from feeding our men."[181]

Dr. Curtis also attested to the difficult travels in a letter home, writing that this segment of the excursion was just "one stinking Traitor hole from Elmira to Harrisburg." Curtis added that Elmira, New York, was

> *one of the meanest towns on the footstool.... They refused to give us anything to eat & went so far as to say that ours was no regiment & came very near getting themselves into Hot Water for if they had not of furnished something we should have taken it & they could not have helped themselves. It was a U.S. post & plenty of Grub on hand & would have taken it if we had to fight for it. Well after a while we squeezed quantity of pork, Coffee, & other rations out of them & then came the tug of war.*[182]

Baltimore, Maryland, was a refreshing welcome for the men of the 1st Michigan. Arriving to the depot at 7:00 a.m., the men marched about two miles, after which they were served a hearty breakfast that was prepared for them by the Baltimore Union Relief Association, an organization founded by notable local women. The men said that this was the first substantial evidence of loyalty and friendship they had received since leaving Cleveland. The breakfast consisted of cold meat, bread and hot coffee. This was especially tasty given that the men were recently eating the regular army ration of hardtack and salt pork on their travels.[183] While in Baltimore, the regiment received many positive comments for their good behavior and soldierly appearance. A report on the regiment in *Detroit Advertiser & Tribune* noted, "Baltimore, it is true, shed the first union blood; but she has redeemed herself long since by her kindness to our Union soldiers." The regiment continued its march through Baltimore, parading through the principal streets, after which they boarded a steamship for Annapolis, traveling three hours along the eastern coast.[184]

Later that afternoon, around 5:00 p.m., the men of the 1st Michigan Colored Regiment arrived in Annapolis, where it was storming badly. The regiment disembarked the vessel and marched about three miles into the countryside. Due to the heavy rain, Lieutenant Colonel Bennett made the request for the men to stay inside one of the vacant barracks nearby. The officer in charge of the site denied Bennett's request, stating that it "might cause a disturbance among the white troops stationed there." Despite the harsh weather and sleeping on the cold, hard ground without tents or gum blankets in the rain and four inches of snow during the early hours of the morning, the men "bore it like veterans." The officers found quarters with other colored regiments lying nearby. Dr. Curtis said that the men were all drenched with water but were in good spirits. The men of the regiment received tents at about noon the following day—the officers received wall tents, and the enlisted men were issued small tents, likely shelter tents.[185]

While most of the soldiers slept on the ground in these tents, some of the staff and officers had slightly better conditions. Dr. Curtis described these conditions in a letter home:

> *Just imagine to yourself in a tent 12 x 14 with mother earth for a carpet. Our tent contains two beds made by driving four crotches in the ground and laying poles on for side pieces then cross pieces & on top & on top of that we have placed pine brush & on that our blankets making a fine & comfortable bed. And we are enjoying our camp life as well as could be expected of men who are far distant from their family. But when we think that we may soon be able to return to our loved ones.*

By nightfall, all the tents were up and in "ship shape," creating an encampment they named "Camp Chandler," likely after Michigan's great war senator Zachariah Chandler.[186]

A report from the regiment in the *Detroit Advertiser & Tribune* had this to say:

> *It was a happy day for us when we left old Camp Ward, with its many unpleasant associations, Canada skedadlers, black-hearted recruiting officers, and other things too numerous to mention. We are now far removed from all those pernicious Copperhead influences which have so long injured us as a regiment, and henceforth it will be our aim to keep our record clear and try to honor the State whose name we bear. Our camp is christened in honor of the man who has been firm friend to the vigorous prosecution of the war, and whose voice in tones of thunder rang out in the Senate of our nation, in condemnation of the weak and ruinous campaign of McClellan—Mr. Chandler.*[187]

After several days still in command of the regiment in Annapolis, Colonel Henry Barns officially separated from the 1st Michigan Colored Regiment, being honorably discharged on April 12, 1864.[188] However, Henry Barns, now a civilian, stayed with the regiment for another month, making his way back north from South Carolina on May 13.[189] Prior to leaving Detroit, Barns wrote the following resignation letter on March 23, 1864, to Major Charles Foster of the Bureau for U.S. Colored Troops:

Zachariah Chandler (1813–1879) was a U.S. senator from Michigan, a staunch abolitionist and a key leader in the Republican Party who played a significant role in supporting the Union during the Civil War and during the Reconstruction era. *Library of Congress.*

Major,

I expect to leave here on Monday evening next with my regiment to take it to Annapolis, and I respectfully tender the resignation of my Commission and connection with it, to take effect that time or at such time thereafter as my successor may be appointed and take the command. I leave the day to be named by you, expressing the hope that Captain Chipman will be at Annapolis to take command, on or soon after the arrival of the regiment at Annapolis.

Respectively,
Your ob't servant
H. Barnes
Col. 1st Mich Col[d] Regiment[190]

Three days following Colonel Barns's resignation, Henry Laurens Chipman, a captain in the regular army, was commissioned colonel of the regiment. The West Point graduate and recent veteran of the Battle of Gettysburg (in the year prior to his appointment in the 1st) was a civil engineer and banker before enlisting in the 2nd Michigan Infantry. He served in several units in both the volunteer and regular army. The officers and enlisted men would go on to admire their new colonel.[191] Captain Wilbur Nelson remarked that Chipman "seems to be a first rate drill master" in his first impression of the colonel.[192]

On April 12, 1864, the 1st Michigan Colored Regiment was given special orders from the War Department, informing it that it had been assigned to the 9th Corps, which was under the command of General Burnside.[193] While the men were stationed in Annapolis, the weather continued to be cold and wet. However, that did not slow Michigan's colored regiment down. The men continued to sharpen their skills in preparation for future combat with the Rebels daily. Their proficiency in drill continued to impress those around them. William W. Fish of the 11th New Hampshire Infantry wrote about his sight of the regiment, "There is a colored Regiment, the 1st Michigan Colored Volunteers with a colored band attached. They make good looking soldiers, handle the musket well, and make a good appearance on dress parade."[194]

When the regiment first arrived to the city on its way to the countryside, a reporter for the *American Citizen* newspaper witnessed the regiment passing by and had this to say: "I observed marching through to their encampment, the 1st Michigan (colored) regiment; they marched to good music of a brass band of their own color; they carried the good old flag of the Stars and Stripes, on one side of which I read, 'Presented by the Soldiers Aid Society of Detroit,' on the other: 'All men are born free and equal, to realize which we fight.' Very much moved by the motto on beautiful presentation banner of the Michigan regiment."

The reporter went on to share his thoughts:

> *As I looked upon the forms, many of whom had once worn the white man's chains, but now carried the musket to defend the white man's Government, who once were slaves under the flag they now rally to defend, who but a few years ago had "no rights a white man was bound to respect," but now who now volunteer to defend the rights of all, and are welcomed to the noble defense of the government of our fathers, whose motto they have inscribed upon their banner, to realize which they fight. I*

could only say, "truly the change is great" and if it be a crime for a white man to assail that flag and that motto, certainly it is a noble act in the black man to defend it. "The world moves" onward. "Error and decay" are synonymous terms, and that which is not right must cease to exist, for "God reigns." Rebellion against free institutions must end in its own overthrow, and in the glorious triumph of that flag, and that motto, for "the service of God is perfect freedom."

When the discoverer of our country declared this planet to be round, he but told a truth of nature, which nothing but the hand of God can change. When Roger Williams declared amid the forest of the new world, that "All men had a right to worship God according to the dictates of their own concience," he but declared a truth of God's moral Government, which shall only cease to be a right, when man shall cease to have a conscience or God in existence. And when our venerable Fathers declared that "All men are created free and equal," they only expressed a simple truth of God's creation, which all the tyrants in the world can never erase, and all the rebellions on earth can never overthrow, but this immortal truth, a star of hope shall forever glitter upon that,

Flag of the free hearts only home,
By angel hands to valor given;
Thy echoes are from yonder dome,
And all thy words were born in heaven.
Forever float that model sheet,
Where breathes the Reb, but falls before us,
With freedom soil beneath our feet,
And freedoms motto floating over us.

"To Realize which we fight," was the impulse of our noble sires, and by their valor, suffering and perseverance during seven years warfare, they secured for our realization the liberty we enjoy and gave into our hands this blood-stained charter of universal freedom. Let it be inscribed upon the banners and hearts of all. Let it never pass from our hands except as a rich and untarnished legacy to our children. Let that motto of God's creation be inscribed upon our banners until it becomes a living reality, acknowledged and realized by all, then rebellion against this law of nature's God, will be unknown. All will be free, all will be equal, all will be peace, all will be happy; none will wear crowns, none will bear arms, none will live in chains. And then it will be the glory of America, that she has been the

asylum for the oppressed. The birthplace of Civil and Religious Liberty. The Cradle of Human Freedom, and the grave of Human Slavery. "To realize which we fight."[195]

While drill was one of the most important and common things the soldiers did on a daily basis in camp, they also had quite a bit of downtime for other activates, especially in poor weather. Having time to step away from medical duties, Dr. Curtis described his creation of a new table for the mess:

Well Dear Friends we have been to work to day engaged in preparing a table for our mess. It may not exceed in beauty some of the Rosewood yet we think it quite a pretty thing. Let me give you an Idea how we made it. In the first place we drove four posts into the ground cutting off the top of the posts about the usuall height for a table. Then we get two poles as streight as can be found & place them on the nailing them on the top of the poles. This makes a frame about 6 or 8 feet in length by 3 in width. We cover this with the remains of a pine box and this makes our table. You ask what next. Why we take a clean bed tick and spread it on the table and then it is ready for the dishes. We have a sett of Tin plates cups &c. These we put in or on the table and then we call for our grub which consists of Beef Steak Potatoes Oysters Bread & Butter Coffee & other to mention. We get oysters for 20cts a qu & just from their shell. Don't you wish you wish you could just step into our hotel & take dinner and though you think it may not be very funny but our officers enjoy themselves quite well![196]

At Camp Chandler, the men of the 1st Michigan Colored Regiment were also treated to a pet dog named "Major." The men called him the "Regimental Pup." This pet belonged to Dr. Curtis, who said that the dog was

getting quite Savage & will growl nights if he hears anything about our camp. He will make a terrible fuss if he is disturbed while eating. Has left the marks of his teeth on several of them who have troubled him while eating his ration of beef which his master had procured for him. On the whole I think my Major can not be surpassed. You see he is part English Masttiff & Newfoundland. The first one of the most savage & the Strongest of all Dog kind. The second is noted for their sagacity [and] *kind nature & I know my Dog poseses both all of these qualities. You may laugh at my enthusiasm over my dog but when you consider that he is my bed fellow &*

> *in a measure my only companion you will not wonder at my friendship & if I do not have the misfortune to lose him you may expect to have my dog with him me!*[197]

On the morning of April 14, 1864, a soldier from headquarters in Washington, D.C., brought a dispatch to Camp Chandler ordering the regiment's commanders to be "in readiness to fall in line of battle on shortage," seemingly indicating that a review of the regiment was to be had that day. This order created a busy scene in the camp, which had been quiet of late. Contingents of officers and enlisted men speculated on what would be the need for such an action on short notice. Was this going to be the day of their first battle? Piercing the rumors, Lieutenant Colonel William T. Bennet officially announced to the men that they were to be reviewed by the commander of the Union army, Lieutenant General Ulysses S. Grant.[198]

The 1st Michigan Colored Regiment was formed into line in a brief matter of time, standing firm and "still as the breeze, but dreadful as the storm." Shortly after getting into formation, men riding on horseback arrived—more than one famous commanding general in fact. As they got close, several of the men quickly recognized Major General Burnside in attendance with Grant as well, adding more importance to the inspection. The esteemed generals, along with their staff, rode along the lines, scrutinizing all of the officers very closely. A reporter from the *Detroit Advertiser & Tribune* standing close by overheard General Burnside say, "General, they look fine." General Grant simply replied, "Splendid." The Detroit reporter added that the general "can recognize discipline and merit in the soldier, black or white. With such a man to lead us, the armies of the Union I firmly believe will soon wipe out the vestige of treason and rebellion, and restore peace and harmony to our distracted country."[199]

Finally continuing its way down to the front lines of the conflict, the 1st Michigan Colored Regiment packed and prepared for its journey down the coast to Hilton Head, South Carolina, on April 14, 1864.[200] The following day, the regiment boarded transports on the water to make its way down the Chesapeake Bay into the Atlantic. At 5:00 p.m., the men rode aboard three transports, *Viz Relief*, *North Point* and *Nellie Pentz*, the latter of which was a 409-ton side-wheel paddle steamer. The staff, along with Companies A and F, were put on the *Relief*; Companies C, D and I were on the *North Point*; and Companies E, H, K, B and G were on the *Nellie Pentz*. About 10:00 a.m. the following day, they passed the famed Fortress Monroe and Rip Raps. Dr. Curtis described the ride as "not so pleasant at times": "Outside the capes, the sea was very rough & then we began to experience all the horrors of sea sickness and many a one rendered up their accounts to old Neptune for the first time & I can assure you that your humble servant was not behind the rest!"[201] Private Murray wrote his own account of the voyage, saying, "The first knight was rough. Sometime we thought we would go down to the bottom."[202]

Sickness wasn't the only opponent they faced on the water, as they soon came in contact with an unknown vessel. On the morning of the seventeenth, a ship was reported on their bows; they watched it with great interest. The ship came within three miles of them, at which point it sent a shot across their bows to inform transport that they were wanted. The engines of the *Nellie Pentz* came to a stop, and they sat quietly at rest on the water. There was a great amount of speculation among the regiment as to who the unknown vessel was. All looked with anxious eyes at the ship until it came near enough for them to see the glorious Stars and Stripes, which hung at its mast. The vessel proved to be the U.S. steam gunboat *Quaker City*, a heavy, 1,451-ton ship fitted with a powerful twenty-pounder cannon.[203]

The regiment arrived at Hilton Head, South Carolina, at about noon on April 19, 1864, and marched about a mile out of the city, where it set up camp.[204] Just over a week later, the men received their long-awaited payroll. However, most of the men, particularly in Company I, refused to sign their names to receive pay at the rate of ten dollars per month. Certainly, the colored soldiers felt that receiving lower pay than "a slave wage" was an insult. Many refused taking any pay at all. Captain Wilbur Nelson of Company I wrote, "I advised them to take what they could get but they appeared set in their determination."[205]

Black soldiers during the Civil War were paid less than white soldiers, who were paid a wage of $13 per month. However, there is more to this; of the $10 a colored soldier received each month, $3 was withheld for clothing, making the base pay only $7. Even the clothing allowance was less than the $3.50 for white soldiers, which came on top of the $13. The government's rationale for paying Black men less was that the only rate of pay authorized under the amendment of the Militia Act, which allowed their enlistment, was the $10 less $3 for clothing authorized for contrabands. Officers objected nearly as much as the men due to the impact on morale, the inability to pay NCOs more and the ability to charge men for losing gear or disciplinary infractions. Eventually, Congress did right by the men and equalized pay for USCT soldiers.[206] Dr. Curtis described the change: "By this steamship we received good news that congress has passed a law paying

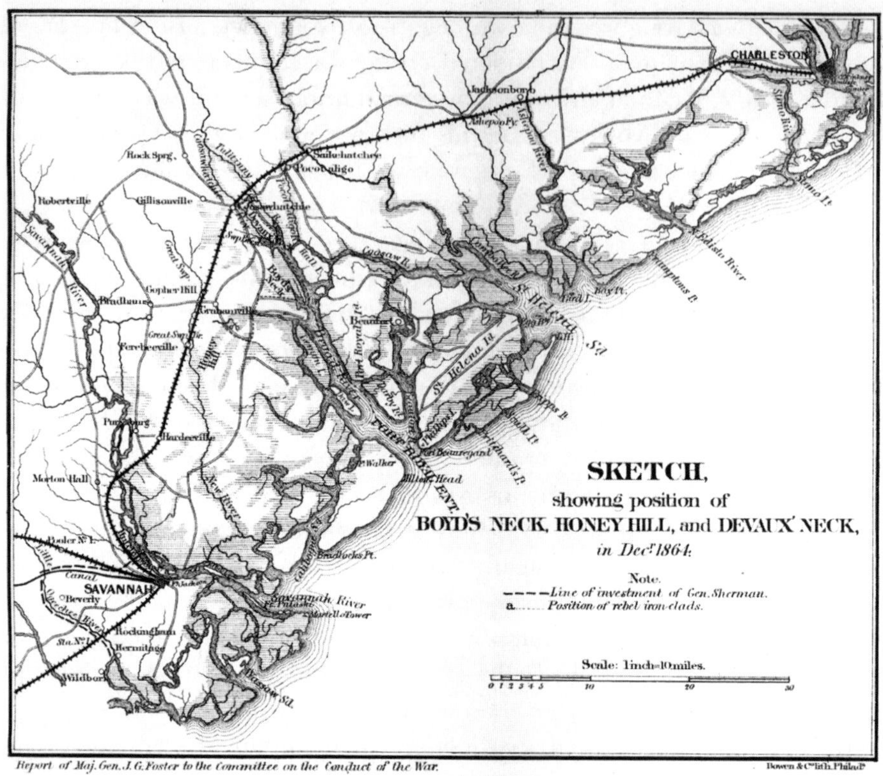

Sketch showing position of Boyd's Neck, Honey Hill and Deveaux's Neck in December 1864. *Library of Congress.*

free colored Troops the same as white Troops. Never did our country pass a more just law than this! If they leave home & friends for the field no man but a contemptable Copperhead will ever object to it."[207]

The 1st Michigan Colored Regiment was assigned to garrison duty in the area and drilled on how operate both light and heavy artillery, which was important in the area since it was along the coastline, where the fortifications were armed with cannons.[208] The Rebels attempted to plant some batteries on a point of land on the opposite side of the channel from the 1st Michigan Colored Regiment's position on the island, but the Union gunboats "drove them double quick from the position!" There were also several other colored regiments nearby that the men were brigaded with for a period of time: the 9th USCT and the 35th USCT. Now, given this was the South, there was a notable difference in the weather and land, which Dr. Curtis described in a letter home:

The weather is very warm now about like our July at home so you may judge how warm it is here and we feel the effects of the heat more on accounts of the camping ground being one complete bed of sand and so fine at that as to be as disagreeable as fine snow when the wind blows. Just imagine to your self a camp upon a bed of sand as fine as corn meal and the wind blowing like the ___ and just think what fun we have. If you face it you run the risk of losing his peepers & if he turns his back upon it he will have a fine job brushing up dress parade.... We have to use no black pepper here for every breeze that would lift a feather has enough of fine sea sand to season the plate of food. We think we shall be able to eat our allowance of dirt (a peck) before we leave the Island![209]

The temperature was recorded to be eighty-six degrees in the shade during the month of May.[210] With the wool uniforms, it likely felt even warmer. However, as they were on the coast, there was at least a friendly breeze from the ocean. The heat eventually reached over one hundred degrees, preventing the men from drilling between the hours of 7:00 a.m. and 7:00 p.m. The sandy, tropical location also came with bugs. Private Murray discussed how scorpions would sometimes run the whole length of his body and that the "sand fleas are thicker than oyster shells."[211]

Dr. Curtis, now having spent several months with the regiment, certainly had an increased positive change of perspective of and strong relationship with the colored soldiers. Learning of the recent tragic battle in Tennessee where Nathan Bedford Forrest, future founding member of the Ku Klux Klan, attacked Fort Pillow and brutality slaughtered about three hundred colored soldiers, Curtis wrote the following home:

You will hear long before you get this of the massacre of troops at Fort Pillow and also at Plymouth North Carolina last week. If this does not awake Old Abe from his lethargy and cause a stop to be put on that barbarous practice. If he does not do something before long he will forfeit the respect of true and loyal men and never more seat himself in the Presidential Chair. How in Gods name can he sit in Washington and see innocent men, women & children murdered in cold blood because the color of their skin is black. If old Abe wishes for them (his soldiers) to take the matter into their own hands they will not wait long for it makes their blood boil and if they make one more for the purpose of retribution it be unto the Rebs a Hell let loose. God forgive the crimes that will be perpetrated by our colored Troops at such a time. Did I say they would perpetrate a crime. No it would only be justice.[212]

Much of the service time on the front lines for Michigan's colored regiment would be spent doing picket duty or outpost duty and manual labor, which tended to be common for colored soldiers during the war. This led to minimal contact with the enemy while still on the front lines. Unfortunately, the regiment was also split apart by company for much of the service as well, separating the men from their Wolverine State brothers. Not long after arriving at Hilton Head, Companies E and F were ordered to pack up and sent on a boat for Seabrook. For the foreseeable future, all companies of the regiment would engage in picket duty near Hilton Head, St. Helena Island, Jenkins Island, Seabrook and Spanish Wells before being sent to Port Royal.[213]

This area of the region was on the other side of the island roughly eight miles from the camp and the rest of their regiment. Private Murray described being on picket duty, noting that they could see the Rebels in the distance, and they could see as a fortification was struck by shells and captured. However, they were not ordered to advance or patriciate in this engagement. Private Murray described picket duty as "lazy work," adding, "We have no drill. All we do is lay around and about 5 o'clock is inspection of arms....Stewed Beef and Coofee and harde tack for breakfast." Company drills and inspections were common for the regiment. Aiming to keep the regiment disciplined and

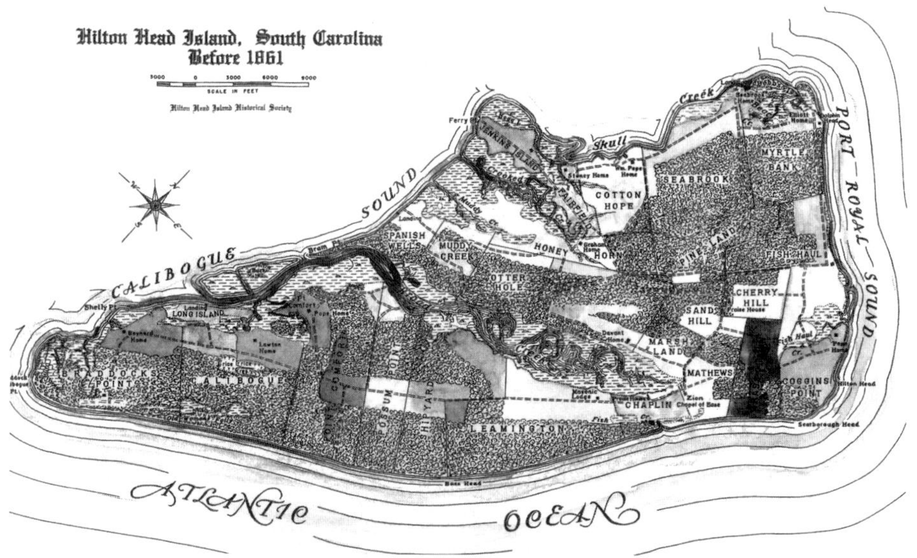

Map of Hilton Head Island, South Carolina, in 1861. *Library of Congress.*

in pristine condition, Colonel Chipman issued an order in the month prior for the officers of the regiment to inspect the enlisted men's arms, clothing and accoutrements daily to ensure that they were good shape.[214]

The *Detroit Advertiser & Tribune* reporter embedded with the 1st Michigan Colored Regiment reported that Companies D, E and F of the 1st Michigan were stationed at Seabrook Landing, South Carolina, conducting picket duty under Major Houghton of the 25th Ohio Regiment. Unlike many other regiments, the 25th Ohio showed less prejudice toward the colored troops; their camps were positioned close together, separated by only a single street. The reporter noted that while the regiment's headquarters remained at the entrenchments at Hilton Head, the 1st Michigan was dispersed across various posts on the islands. This separation, the reporter observed, diminished the regiment's ability to maintain cohesive drill and discipline.[215]

Private John Murray of the regiment described leaving Sea Brook to rejoin the regiment at Hilton Head, where all the companies were gathered once more. Now stationed at the fort, Murray's company was drilling with heavy artillery; he described the guns as being more than fourteen feet long and capable of firing sixty-four-pound shells, with the men using nothing but grape and canister shot.[216] In addition, they were constructing other fortification within an existing one, with his estimate of seven hundred colored soldiers and one thousand white soldiers to build it—a structure spanning nearly three-quarters of a mile made entirely of sand from the sea. The boys said, "Spades are trumps, and they all hold a good hand."[217] Despite no immediate threat, the troops stayed vigilant, prepared for any potential danger. Murray also expressed a preference for picket duty over being confined within the fort, hinting at the anticipation among the men for a possible encounter with Confederate forces. "If the Rebs call on us," he wrote, "we'll meet them halfway." Just recently, they had detained two white spies and some others, bringing them to shore after discovering that their passes were invalid. These captives were then escorted to headquarters. Each day, they witnessed gunboats in the area firing at the enemy whenever they spotted groups of Confederate soldiers, often shelling them twice a day.[218]

While the regiment was often split apart, the companies typically stayed within range of their brethren. Dr. Curtis described this in a letter home: "We have only two companys left here in camp. The other 8 are on detached service some in one place & some in another. we have two companys acting as garrison in the Fort, two here, one on St Helena Island & three at Spanish Wells, two at Sea brook all within a circle of 15 miles!" While in this region,

Photograph showing a Union soldier standing next to a heavy artillery cannon at Fort Welles, formally Fort Walker. *New Hampshire Historical Society*.

several companies of the 1st Michigan Colored Regiment, particularly companies I and K, were moved to occupy Fort Welles alongside the 9th United States Colored Troops. Originally names Fort Walker, this fort was built with the labor of slaves during 1861. The fortification was constructed to shield Port Royal against a Union blockade. This was the location of one of the South's most important commerce ports. However, the newly built fort fell to Union forces in November 1861 during the Battle of Port Royal. Following the battle, it was renamed Fort Welles (after Secretary of the Navy Gideon Welles). It wouldn't be long until the 9th United States Colored Troops would move out of the fort, with Colonel Chipman being placed in command of the coast and his full regiment occupying Fort Welles.[219]

At this time, not much was spoken of racial tensions between the white soldiers and civilians. However, the men of the regiment did bring attention to some tensions between the Black soldiers of the regiment and the local contrabands. The less fortunate and educated colored contrabands and civilians would at times despise the enlisted soldier of the 1st Michigan Colored. Dr. Curtis saw such interactions happening between the colored men and wrote, "The general run of the contrabands are the most degraded

Photo of Fort Walker/Wells in 1861. *Library of Congress.*

of all human being you can hardly understand one of them. They hate a Yonkey Nigger as they call our boys because they think our boys feel above them. But they learn very fast. There are children here who six months ago did not know their letters are now working sums on the blackboard. You may think this strange but it is nevertheless true!"[220] Contrabands were typically formerly enslaved colored men who escaped to Union lines, seeking freedom and safety. The term *contraband* was first used by General Benjamin Butler, who, in 1861, declared that escaped enslaved people would be considered "contraband of war" and thus not returned to their owners.[221] With most of these men being former slaves, many of them were not as educated and as well spoken as Dr. Curtis described.

Religion was a significant aspect of life for colored soldiers during the Civil War, providing them with a source of strength and resilience. Many soldiers turned to their faith as they faced the challenges of military life and the fight for freedom. Spirituals, singing and hymns became vital expressions of hope, often reflecting themes of liberation that resonated deeply with their experiences. These songs served not only as morale boosters but also as a means of communication and solidarity among troops. The work of chaplains and religious leaders within the ranks fostered a strong sense of community, offering spiritual guidance and encouraging soldiers to find courage in their shared beliefs.[222]

Additionally, the intersection of faith and military service helped shape the identity and mission of the USCT. Many soldiers viewed their enlistment as part of a divine purpose, believing that they were fighting for both their own liberation and the freedom of future generations. This conviction was reinforced through sermons and religious gatherings in camp, which emphasized the righteousness of their cause and the moral imperative of ending slavery. The emphasis on faith imbued their struggle with a sense of higher significance, motivating them to endure hardships and strive for justice. This powerful blend of faith and purpose created a strong bond among African American soldiers, underscoring the vital role of religion in their fight for freedom.[223]

The chaplain of the 102nd was William Waring, an educated colored man from Oberlin, Ohio. Having a colored member of the regimental staff meant a great deal to the men. Born in 1833 in Virginia, Waring was a dedicated educator, minister and advocate for African American rights.[224] After early education in Pennsylvania and Ohio, he began teaching in 1850 and was ordained as a Baptist minister in 1860. During the Civil War, he served as chaplain to the 102nd, providing spiritual support to soldiers. After the war, he ministered in Ohio and New York, and in 1871, he joined the Sixth Auditor's office in Washington, D.C., where he served until 1899, earning commendations for his work. A passionate community leader, he was instrumental in founding the Capital City Savings Bank and served as the first pastor of Berean Baptist Church. A graduate of Howard University Law School, he authored several unpublished works on race and justice. Waring remained deeply committed to social progress and was a respected Howard University trustee, remembered as a conscientious, broad-minded leader.[225]

Dr. Curtis wrote of a memorable church service held in the improvised chapel that the soldiers had created on the island of Hilton Head. The men had gathered brush from the woods to construct a simple arbor, where boards served as seats for the congregation. On recent Sundays, the location was filled with about 100 to 150 attendees, a diverse gathering of officers, enlisted men and former slaves, all assembled to listen intently to the chaplain's sermon. Many of these soldiers had endured years in bondage before gaining freedom and donning the Federal blue uniform. Dr. Curtis observed that although some of these men were unpolished and uneducated, their faith and sincerity shone through. To him, their devotion was genuine and wholehearted, creating an atmosphere he had never experienced in other worship settings.[226]

In this humble chapel, Dr. Curtis noted, traditional social distinctions faded away. Pride of birth and wealth were set aside, and everyone came together on equal ground, all bound by the same message and purpose. Military etiquette, usually rigidly observed, was relaxed, allowing the men to worship freely and equally. Curtis was moved by the heartfelt prayers offered, many of which centered on the soldiers' struggles and their hopes for liberty. The honesty and depth of these prayers fascinated and inspired him, as he watched these men pray not only for themselves but also for strength to overcome the many trials they faced as soldiers and newly freed men. Dr. Curtis found something profoundly Christian in the faith of these "uneducated mortals" who, though lacking formal religious instruction, seemed to embrace their beliefs with a purity that more educated men often failed to achieve. He noted that these Black regiments, such as the 8th USCT and the famous 54th Massachusetts, went into battle singing and praying with all their might, trusting in their savior to welcome them should they fall. Their battle cry, "God, Liberty, and seven dollars a month," symbolized a cause greater than themselves—a cause of freedom and faith, uniting them in courage and purpose, facing death without fear.[227]

The *Tribune* reporter described a review of the troops on May 24, 1864, conducted by General William Birney, who commanded Hilton Head, Fort Pulaski, St. Helena and Tybee Islands. The reviewed units included the 1st Michigan Colored Regiment, the 9th United States Colored Troops, the 104th Pennsylvania and a Massachusetts cavalry regiment (white). The reporter noted that the 1st Michigan Colored Regiment performed well, matching the appearance and discipline of the other units.[228]

While on the island, the health of the regiment was typically good, but sickness did find its way into the ranks. Several of the men endured diarrhea and dysentery—among the deadliest diseases for Civil War soldiers, fueled by unsanitary camp conditions and contaminated water. Together, these illnesses caused more noncombat deaths than any other ailment, with diarrhea alone killing more than fifty-seven thousand Union soldiers.[229] Treatment options were limited and often ineffective, leaving many soldiers weakened or fatally dehydrated. The widespread illness significantly reduced troop strength, highlighting the dire need for improved sanitation and medical care.[230]

"We are no more the Michigan boys," wrote Private Murray, during the month of May. The War Department had redesignated the 1st Michigan Colored Regiment to the 102nd United States Colored Troops.[231] The officers of the regiment received the order from Washington, D.C., on June 1. The redesignation was due to War Department General Order No. 143, which established a procedure of enlisting African Americans into the armed forces. The order created the Bureau of Colored Troops, which designated African American regiments as United States Colored Troops (USCT).[232] At the time the order went into effect in May 1863, there had been some African American regiments operating under state designations, and there were a few regiments stationed near New Orleans in the Department of the Golf designated as Corps d'Afrique. All of these regiments were folded into the USCT. This different treatment of African American soldiers meant that the 102nd USCT was the only regiment to come out of the state of Michigan to lose its state designation.[233] The *Tribune* reporter expressed his thoughts on the change, writing, "I trust our Michigan friends will not forget us on this account, for we still claim a State indemnity, inspire of this new number."[234]

With the new designation, Private Murray noted that they had a "half a pound of brass" on their head.[235] Civil War soldiers sometimes were issued insignia to wear on their caps to signify their unit and branch of service, helping to establish organization and cohesion within the ranks. Insignia often included numbers, letters or symbols. This system helped to reduce confusion, especially in the large and diverse armies that the Civil War mobilized, where units from different states and backgrounds served together. Additionally, wearing identifiable insignia promoted pride and unity among soldiers, reinforcing a sense of belonging and loyalty to their specific regiment or division. The visual markers served practical and symbolic purposes, solidifying both structure and morale on the battlefield.[236]

One positive aspect the men found for this new designation was that it helped ensure that their mail would arrive to correct regiment. Around this time, in mid-June, Dr. Curtis explained that many men were having issues getting mail back from home, as their letters would end up in the hands of other Michigan regiments. This was because several regiments mustered out of the state with their regimental number beginning with "1st." This was also a problem for the other regiments. Dr. Curtis wrote, "We have received at our camp since we came into S.C. letters from the north belonging to the 1st Mich S.S., 1 Mich. Infantry & 1st Mich Cavalry &c so it is obvious to me that our letters have gone to them."[237]

Mail from loved ones at home was a vital lifeline for soldiers on the front, providing much-needed emotional support amid the hardships of battle and camp life. Letters offered a connection to home, reminding soldiers of their families and communities and boosting morale in an otherwise isolating and grueling environment. These messages helped to sustain hope, strengthen resolve and give soldiers a reason to endure the challenges they faced each day. In a letter to be sent back home, Dr. Curtis shared his impatient excitement to see if he received a letter from his wife in Michigan, writing, "Well Amelia, Yesterday afternoon Dr's V & S & myself went to the town for a walk and called at Post Office and got the mail bag. we came out as far as a grove just out of the city and could wait no longer for we wanted to see the news. well we poured the contense on the ground and began the search and as a reward for our labor I found five letters from you & one from Cousin Charles."[238]

In the camp of the regiment, one could find number of dedicated women who took on the mission of educating the colored soldiers, recognizing the transformative power of literacy for formerly enslaved and free colored men alike. These women, often referred to as "school marms," organized classes in reading, writing and arithmetic, seeing education as essential for the soldiers' personal empowerment and future as citizens. Their work sometimes occurred in makeshift classrooms within the camps, where they not only taught basic literacy skills but also helped instill a sense of dignity and hope among the soldiers.[239]

Many of these teachers faced criticism and hostility, as educating colored men was seen by some as controversial or even subversive in that era. Yet figures like Charlotte Forten, a free colored woman and teacher from the North, persevered, working tirelessly among the soldiers of the 1st South Carolina Volunteers (colored) on the Sea Islands; she documented her experiences and the soldiers' eagerness to learn.[240] Other teachers were backed by organizations such as the American Missionary Association, which provided resources and support for literacy efforts among freedmen and soldiers. Their contributions left a lasting impact, as these soldiers, equipped with the tools of literacy, were better prepared to advocate for their rights and navigate postwar society.[241]

Chapter 17

The 102nd United States Colored Troops

On June 15, 1864, the men of the 102nd United States Colored Troops were relieved from their duty at Fort Welles, with the 3rd Rhode Island Infantry taking over the garrison. Nearing the midnight hour that evening, the regiment commenced with tearing down its tents to make its way to Beaufort, South Carolina. Marching to the beach the following morning, the regiment boarded the steamboat *Cosmopolitan*. The sail up the river was reported to be pleasant, and the men discussed passing plantations in the distance that were once owned by slave owners and were now managed by Black Union soldiers. Arriving at Beaufort, the regiment marched about a half mile to the rear of the town to make camp.[242]

While many soldiers were ill from sickness, Dr. Curtis explained that he found many colored soldiers of the regiment coming to his tent for less important matters:

> *It is a fact that Colored men who have been brought up at the north can not stand the hot climate like our Northern White men. they have not the ambition that supports the white soldier in his adversitys. if they have a pain in their big toe they want an excuse and a great many things that a white soldier would blush to come before a Surgeon and ask for an excuse! They want the Stamina of white men. they are easily discouraged and when one of them are sick they give up and have no more ambition than a beast yet some of them will work until they are very sick before they will give up!*[243]

On June 23, the regiment was reviewed and inspected by General Edward Potter, who was its brigade commander in the region. Captain Wilbur Nelson of Company I was not pleased with the turnout. He wrote, "The men made a very poor appearance, they and their guns were dirty. It seems very hard to make anything of these men, I am about discouraged." Days later, the 1st Michigan Colored Regiment received orders to join an expedition expected to encounter Confederate forces. As they had long awaited their time to fight, this news filled the camp with excitement. Even men who had been excused from duty due to illness were found preparing their guns, determined to participate despite their condition.[244] However, this anticipation turned to disappointment when, only hours later, a countermanding order arrived. The regiment learned that it would instead be assigned double duty, guarding the city and nearby fortifications, as concerns about their condemned weapons led higher command to deem them unfit for combat against the Rebels. Brigadier General Potter, commanding the brigade, reportedly expressed his regret, stating that he "would like very much to have that splendid Michigan regiment along, but 'twould be suicide to take them with their worthless guns." While disappointed, the men knew the reality to be true, for two-thirds of the rifles had to snap a cap nearly a dozen times before the black powder would ignite, triggering the explosion sending the projectile down range.[245]

This matter of poor firearms frustrated the soldiers, who felt confident that they could still serve on the expedition effectively, even if armed only with their bayonets. The men held on to the promise of replacement weapons soon, hoping to finally join their comrades on the battlefield. They carried Austrian Lorenz muskets purchased in 1861 by General Frémont, weapons long condemned by Secretary of War Simon Cameron. Eager to receive proper arms, they wished to be freed from what felt like "eternal guarding" and picket duties while others earned accolades in battle. Despite this setback, the men took pride in their reputation, praised as "splendid guards" and "trusty pickets." The regiment remained determined to prove itself, with a reporter concluding, "We shall yet have a name, a proud one, too, for our fighting qualities. Michigan shall yet be proud of us."[246]

The discussion behind the men having poor weapons was not new. In fact, Private Murray mentioned his dissatisfaction with the arms on reaching the East Coast. In the last quarter of 1863, while in Detroit, the regiment was issued its Lorenz muskets, and by the fourth quarter of 1864, the men finally received new weapons, which were Springfield rifles Models 1855, 1861 and 1863, all .58 caliber, along with a substantial supply of more Lorenz muskets equipped with leaf and block sights and quadrangular bayonets, also .58 caliber. Other regiments using similar weapons reported no particular issues, suggesting that the mention of "poor guns" may have applied to a certain company within the regiment or perhaps was a misreported detail. It's also possible that the Springfields and Austrian muskets provided were defective or that the regiment initially departed Detroit with substandard arms not officially recorded.[247]

At this point in early July, the men started to notice the increasing number of deaths in the ranks. In just the first nine days of July 1864 alone, ten men of the regiment had died. One of those dead was twenty-four-year-old Henry Dimond Benham, who had died from dysentery. A graduate of Michigan State Agricultural College in 1861, he initially enlisted as a sergeant in Company D of the 7th Michigan Cavalry and fought alongside General George Armstrong Custer on the third day at the Battle of Gettysburg. Later, in March 1864, he was commissioned as a first lieutenant in Company B of the 1st Michigan Colored Regiment. His father, Elias P. Benham (1805–1864), who worked as an abolitionist, also served in the same cavalry regiment. It is possible that his father's involvement inspired Henry to join the cause as well. While stationed at Hilton Head, the young lieutenant fell ill with smallpox but continued his duties before fully recovering, despite the doctor's advice against it. This alone might not have worsened his condition, but he later attended a festival in town, where he likely consumed ice cream, wine and other indulgences.[248]

Combined with exposure to South Carolina's intense heat, this led to a severe case of dysentery. The regiment's hospital staff, along with Dr. Curtis, had his illness under control and believed that he might recover, but as soon as he noticed their absence, he instructed his young servant to bring him ice water and other indulgences. Though warned by Dr. Curtis that these would worsen his condition, he persisted until his health declined further, ultimately leading to his passing. He was noted to be a fine young man, well liked by all who knew him. He was laid to rest with both military and Masonic honors at Beaufort National Cemetery, which was in viewing distance of the 102nd USCT's camp in Beaufort.[249]

In his diary, Captain Wilbur Nelson of Company I recounted an afternoon ride with Lieutenant Holmes in South Carolina during which they observed "some black children running about entirely naked" and nearly "came near riding over two little babies rolled up in an old blanket and laid under a tree outdoors." This vivid description highlights the severe poverty and neglect faced by newly emancipated colored families during the Civil War. Despite their freedom, many lacked basic necessities such as clothing and shelter, underscoring the harsh realities of their circumstances. Nelson's account provides a poignant glimpse into the forthcoming challenges of the Reconstruction era, illustrating the profound struggles that accompanied the transition from slavery to freedom.[250]

A letter from Private Murray shed light on the often-strained relations between Northern colored soldiers and those from Southern Union regiments, such as the 2nd South Carolina. Despite fighting under the same Union cause, these regiments sometimes experienced tension, rooted in differing backgrounds and views on service. Murray noted that the Southern troops, formed largely from formerly enslaved men or "contrabands," harbored resentment toward the Northern soldiers, calling them "Black Yan-keys" and accusing them of cowardice. Dr. Curtis had his own opinion, writing that "the contraband Niggers are little above the barbarian."[251]

This friction was exacerbated by perceived favoritism from Union leadership, as the Northern troops were allegedly "showed a little favor" on an expedition, which the Southern Union colored troops saw as an injustice. The clash that followed a verbal dispute between soldiers of the 102nd USCT and the 2nd South Carolina escalated when members of the Southern regiment returned to their quarters to retrieve rifles, prompting soldiers of the 102nd to arm themselves with improvised weapons like clubs and bricks. Despite the heated exchange and physical confrontation, Lieutenant Colonel Bennett reported that the situation was ultimately defused without any serious consequences. These interactions reveal the complex layers of identity, pride and rivalry that existed within the Union's colored regiments, even as they fought for a common goal of freedom and equality. The tension reveals the difficulties of bringing together diverse groups within the Union forces, where a shared racial identity did not necessarily translate into solidarity.[252]

In a letter from the 102nd USCT's encampment in Beaufort, South Carolina, Dr. Curtis described the military camp setup and daily living conditions, giving a vivid image of life in the field. Writing on a "pleasant morning," Curtis invited his family at home to "imagine yourself out in an open field where the tents of several thousand men are encamped." He explained how the camp resembles a small city, with "neat & tidy streets" and each company occupying its own street. The tents of company officers line up behind the troops, followed by the field and staff officers' tents, which stood on platforms about two feet off the ground, measuring roughly ten feet square. Curtis humorously noted that, back home, people "would think you were cramped to death" in such tight quarters.[253]

Describing the modest furnishings in his tent, Curtis wrote that he and Dr. Vincent shared essentials like bunks, a small table between their beds for writing and a makeshift washstand created from an old hardtack box. "Now what do you think of our living in style?" he joked, showing their resourcefulness in making do with limited resources. He also mentioned the "shelter tents," or "dog tents," issued to the men, which barely cover one's head and evoke an image of a chicken hiding from a hawk. Curtis humorously envisioned his friend Frank's "long legs twisting to get into one of them," giving readers a lighthearted view of the daily challenges and camaraderie within the camp.[254]

On July 31, 1864, the enlisted men of the regiment finally received orders prepare to advance farther into the South, likely to engage the enemy. This news was exciting but was also met with great worry. That evening, the men packed up their encampment and shared their emotions with one another. One of the largest worries was that the men had not yet been supplied with new weapons. Men like Private Murray felt that if they were to be engaged in this coming movement, he would be slaughtered.[255] The next morning, prior to leaving Beaufort, a more positive and celebratory feeling was in the air, August 1 marked an important day of celebration and reflection for Black communities in the United States during the 1860s. Known as West Indian Emancipation Day, it commemorated the abolition of slavery in the British West Indies on August 1, 1834.[256]

For free Black Americans, particularly those in Northern states, this day was a powerful reminder of the progress achieved toward freedom and a symbol of the work still to be done to end slavery within the United States. Gatherings took place in large cities where parades, church services and speeches fostered a sense of unity and purpose. Prominent figures, including Frederick Douglass, used these celebrations to deliver stirring addresses that connected the plight of Black Americans with global movements for liberation, calling for a collective commitment to abolishing slavery in the United States. As the Civil War unfolded, these gatherings took on new significance, with attendees expressing hope that the Union's struggle might lead to freedom for enslaved people in the Southern states.[257]

During the 102nd USCT's celebration, several soldiers delivered stirring speeches of their own. In perfect timing with the festive occasion, the regiment arrived in Hilton Head, where they were issued new rifles, a moment that filled the men with excitement and pride.[258]

The following day, on August 2, 1864, the regiment left South Carolina aboard a steamship for Jacksonville, Florida, arriving the following day, where they stayed overnight. Supplied with seven days' worth of rations, the 102nd proceeded into enemy lines; the men would go to Baldwin, about twenty miles along the Florida Railroad, enduring intense heat and challenging conditions in the low, swampy, desolate landscape. Baldwin itself was a small railroad station with just a few old houses. Alligators were thick in the surrounding swamps, and frogs serenaded the men nightly, adding an eerie atmosphere to their stay in the hostile terrain. In this section of the railroad, the 102nd received orders to destroy the tracks, preventing their use by Confederate forces. The men dismantled approximately three miles, burning the ties and bending the rails to render them unusable. Additional regiments from Beaufort participating in this operation included the 29th Connecticut Infantry (Colored), the 9th USCT, the 26th USCT and the 34th USCT.[259]

During its time so far in service, the regiment's only combat with the Rebels had been through skirmishing, which often consisted of small numbers of soldiers doing picket firings. Private Murray wrote about a skirmish with the enemy he was involved with during his first few days in Florida:

> *We Squrmishing most all knight with them. they thought they could Drive us in the Same they Did the first South. they found out it could not Be Don. they Did not Drive us nor twice the number. what Johnny got to Do he Dost in hurray and off. I had A Ball Split the wood on my Gun and Cut Into I had tied on my Back. my Dog tent fell to the ground. the Bullet whistle Around my head like hail Stone. we gave them one Volley. they left to Parts Unknown. we took five Prisoner we would Riddle with Ball if our Cornal would let us. he want us to set Example for them not Disgrace our Self By killing them. I want Revenge what they have Don at fourt Pillow.*[260]

Just under a year since recruiting first started for the Michigan colored regiment, the 102nd finally faced its first real engagement with Confederate forces. On August 10, 1864, the men were conducting their assigned task of dismantling sections of railroad tracks roughly six miles from Baldwin, aiming to disrupt Confederate supply lines and troop movements. As they began their work, a force of Confederate cavalry launched a sudden assault, firing into the regiment's left flank in an attempt to defend the railroad and

The Baldwin area of northern Florida features a mix of pine flatwoods, dense hardwood hammocks and cypress swamps, with sandy, well-drained soil in the higher areas and wetter, swampy lowlands. The terrain is largely flat, with open forests and occasional marshy areas, supporting a variety of plant and animal life adapted to these unique ecosystems. *Florida Family Nature.*

maintain control of Baldwin as a strategic point. Using their familiarity with the swampy terrain, the Confederate cavalry executed a swift ambush to slow the Union soldiers' progress.[261]

Despite the surprise attack, the officers of the 102nd quickly deployed skirmishers, and the regiment successfully repelled the Confederate force without suffering any casualties. Although new to combat, the men of the 102nd displayed impressive resilience and bravery, holding their ground and demonstrating discipline under fire. This brief yet intense engagement tested the regiment's ability to operate effectively in hostile territory and underscored their determination to fulfill their mission. While a small skirmish in the broader scope of the Civil War, the encounter marked a defining moment for the 102nd USCT. Its success not only established it as a capable fighting unit but also challenged the doubts about Black soldiers' effectiveness voiced by publications like the *Detroit Free Press*. This victory strengthened their growing reputation within the Union army, affirming the contributions and courage of Black soldiers in the fight for freedom.[262]

On August 15, 1864, the regiment set out on a multi-day march, covering nearly eighteen miles each day and camping at each stop along the way. Deep within Confederate territory, tension was high. One night, a sudden commotion outside their shelter tents sent a wave of fear through the men as they braced for what they believed was an impending ambush by Rebel cavalry. To their relief, the source of the noise turned out to be nothing more than a herd of cattle rushing past. Nonetheless, the soldiers' vigilance was warranted given the risks of enemy territory.[263]

After several grueling days and about one hundred miles of marching, the 102nd arrived in Magnolia, Florida, on the St. Johns River at sundown on August 19. Along its journey, it managed to gather sixty colored men, two old guns and ten mules.[264] In a letter from Private Alonzo Reed, he described the tough conditions of the march from Baldwin, covering five days at a pace of five miles per hour. "The sun [was] as hot as any oven," he recounted; he also detailed the rough treatment of a fellow soldier who collapsed, noting how "our major grabbed him by the belt and hit him over the head with his sword, then galloped his horse off and dragged him a half a mile." Reed also mentioned the harsh environment, marching "in mud and water up to our waist."[265]

The regiment's presence in the South provided an unexpected opportunity for many African American men to join its ranks, offering a pathway to freedom and a new beginning. This recruitment was especially impactful in places like Beaufort and later in Florida, where the regiment

Coast of South Carolina from Charleston to Hilton Head. This map includes Fort Walker/Welles. *Library of Congress.*

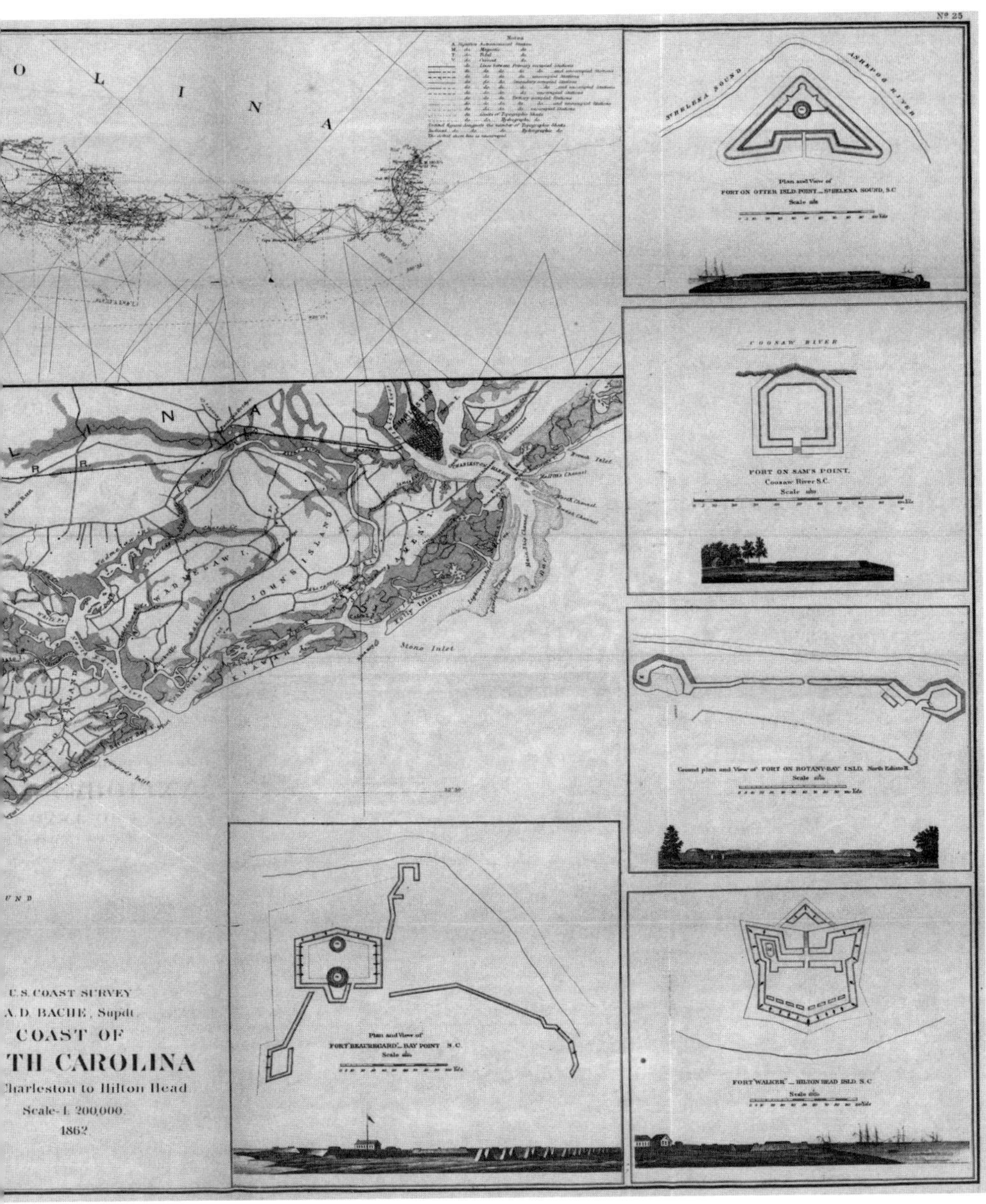
Nº 25
O L I N A
Stono Inlet
Folly Island
JOHNS ISLAND
WADMELAW I.
COOSAW RIVER
FORT ON SAM'S POINT.
Coosaw River S.C.
St HELENA SOUND
ASHEPOO RIVER
Plan and View of
FORT ON OTTER ISLD. POINT__St HELENA SOUND, S.C
Ground plan and View of FORT ON BOTANY-BAY ISLD. North Edisto R.
Plan and View of
FORT "BEAUREGARD"__BAY POINT S.C.
FORT "WALKER"__HILTON HEAD ISLD. S.C
U.S. COAST SURVEY
A.D. BACHE, Supdt.
COAST OF
TH CAROLINA
harleston to Hilton Head
Scale-1: 200,000.
1862.

continued to attract men eager to enlist and fight for the Union cause. The regiment stayed here for ten days doing fatigue duty, which primarily consisted of constructing a fortification in the area. Private Murray described it as such: "Just in camp. very tired. we Been on a March Seven Days. Brought with us in Camp 150 Countreband nine Johnny 17 mules and Six Horses five Big wagons two top Bugges three white women and one girl. Rested two Days and then we Built a heavy fourt of Six Seige Gun. we left Magnolia 29th. arived at Beaufort 31." Upon returning to their former camp in Beaufort, South Carolina, the regiment was split up and performed picket duty in multiple locations over the next few months, including Port Royal, Lady Island and Coosa Island.[266]

Upon returning to the area with little action to occupy them, some soldiers began engaging in offenses both minor and more serious. Late at night on September 27, 1864, Privates William H. Washington and Creed Calloway of the regiment obtained whiskey and became a bit drunk. They went on to cause a disturbance in the soldiers' quarters on the upper floor of the Barnwell Plantation house on Port Royal Island when two sergeants from the regiment tried to calm them down. The privates resisted, ultimately leading to a physical altercation between the soldiers. One common issue was sleeping while on picket duty. Private James Henson and Private Oliver Winslow, both caught sleeping on post, were court-martialed and sentenced to hard labor for the remainder of their enlistments, with a ten-dollar monthly pay deduction. A more severe incident took place weeks later, involving not only soldiers but also local civilians. Privates Bullard, Hardee and Johnson of Company A left camp and went to a nearby plantation, where they allegedly threatened the two women living there. The soldiers reportedly killed several chickens, leaving behind scattered heads, blood and feathers. Although they faced accusations of more serious offenses, the court-martial ultimately convicted them only of being absent without leave, issuing each a ten-dollar fine.[267]

During this time, the 102nd was headquartered at Beaufort, South Carolina. In early October, on the fifth, Confederate forces attempted a surprise assault on the detachment of the regiment stationed at Lady's Island. Under the cover of night, the Rebels planned to land on the island and catch the Union soldiers off guard, hoping to overwhelm them with the element of surprise. However, their approach was detected before they could fully execute their plan. Alerted to the threat, the soldiers of the 102nd swiftly organized a defense and engaged the Confederate attackers. After a quick, fierce and spirited skirmish, the Rebels were unable to penetrate the Union defenses and were ultimately forced to retreat, abandoning their attempted late-night raid on the island.[268]

Later, on October 16, Captain Nelson detailed an encounter in his diary where, in the afternoon, a group of Confederate soldiers in a boat ventured too close to the picket lines. Spotting the approaching Rebels, pickets of the 102nd responded by firing on them, which forced the Confederates to come ashore. As a result, three of the Rebels were taken prisoner. However, one of them attempted to flee, prompting the colored soldiers to fire, with a bullet striking him in the head and killing him instantly. The event underscores the heightened vigilance, accuracy and readiness of regiment to defend their lines against any threat, even small incursions.[269]

Thanksgiving Day on the front lines was marked by a special sermon delivered by Chaplain William Waring at eleven o'clock. The staff officers of the 102nd gathered afterward at headquarters for an exceptional holiday meal, featuring an array of dishes like roast pig, chicken pie, oysters, mashed potatoes, fresh butter, bread and pudding. This abundant spread contrasted with the standard rations and reminded the officers of the comforts of home.[270]

For much of their time stationed in the South, the regiment's staff had enjoyed fresh local foods uncommon in typical army provisions. Being in a subtropical region provided a bounty of produce and ingredients, enriching their meals. They frequently recorded their appreciation of the fresh offerings, listing favorites like green peas, blackberries, lemonade, wine, chicken, turkey, peaches, watermelons, apples, squash, corn, oysters, turnips, cabbage and garden vegetables. Dr. Curtis noted that they were able to enjoy "all the luxuries a man can have at home with the exception of one thing, viz., the society of our friends at home." A cook, a colored woman from Detroit who had joined them, managed the meals for the officers, showcasing her culinary skills honed in large hotels. Curtis described one memorable breakfast of "soft bread, toast, tomatoes, figs just from the tree, coffee & tea, butter."[271]

However, enlisted men of the regiment were often less fortunate, limited to the army's standard ration of salt beef, pork and hardtack. Occasionally, though, they benefited from the region's bounty as well, enjoying fresh foods that were uncommon in other parts of the army. Soldiers reported enjoying tomatoes, peanuts, oranges, watermelon, corn and potatoes. Yet these improvements were intermittent, and they frequently reverted to basic rations—hardtack, cold mule bread and coffee brewed from beans and other "trash." The seasonal and local foods provided welcome breaks from the monotony of army meals, giving them a taste of home amid the challenges of war.[272]

On the morning of November 29 at ten o'clock, Captain Montague led three companies on a march to Hilton Head, where they joined thousands of other Union troops under General Hatch's command. From there, they embarked on ships to meet up with General Foster at Boyd's Landing on the Broad River. Their objective: reach the strategic location of Honey Hill by November 30. Both Union and Confederate forces were aware of the area's importance, as it provided a significant vantage point. However, poor weather, inaccurate maps and unreliable guides hindered the Federal advance, causing a full day's delay.[273]

Confederate General Samuel Jones commanded a local force of about two thousand men, including Georgia militia, two Georgia infantry regiments, the 3rd South Carolina Cavalry and munitions workers from the arsenals in Athens and Augusta. These forces quickly established themselves at Honey Hill, a defensive ridge parallel to the railroad. Jones positioned his troops carefully, with the hill offering an advantageous overlook of swampy ground and dense woods that would restrict Union movement. Additionally, a single road provided the only clear route toward Grahamville and the railroad, and Jones's forces had calibrated their artillery to ensure precise firing distances. Union forces arrived at Boyd's Landing on November 30, five miles from Honey Hill, and started advancing inland. At the same time, Jones prepared his defensive stand on Honey Hill, where reinforcements from Georgia began arriving through the railroad. Colonel Charles Colcock of the 3rd South Carolina Cavalry ordered the grass in front of their line to be set on fire. Wind carried the smoke toward the Union troops, adding confusion and obstructing visibility.[274]

At 11:00 a.m., the battle commenced as Union troops—including the 157th, 56th and 127th New York; 54th and 55th Massachusetts (Colored); 25th Ohio; and the Naval Brigade—engaged the Confederate defenses. Due to the dense woods, Federal artillery could only deploy along the narrow road. Union soldiers struggled to advance through thick underbrush and were picked off by Confederates. The Union artillery expended all its ammunition and was eventually replaced by a naval battery manned by sailors. The 3rd New York Artillery faced heavy losses, with multiple men wounded, transport horses killed and two ammunition chests destroyed. During their retreat, the 3rd New York Artillery was forced to abandon all but one of its cannons.[275]

Captain A.E. Lindsay of the 102nd U.S. Colored Troops was ordered to retrieve the field pieces left by the 3rd New York Artillery. Positioned only

150 yards from Confederate earthworks, the guns lay in a deadly zone within range of enemy fire. Leading his company forward under heavy fire, Captain Lindsay was struck down and killed by the first Rebel volley before reaching the cannons. Command then fell to First Lieutenant Henry Alvord, who was hit by a bullet in his ear and later injured by grapeshot, which drove his sword hook painfully into his side. As he attempted to continue, Alvord was wounded a third time, this time by a musket ball to the back of the head. With both officers incapacitated, command passed to First Sergeant Jesse Madry. Unaware of the mission's objective, Madry, seeing his men suffering heavy casualties, directed the company into the woods to retreat, effectively bringing them out in good order but leaving the guns behind. The severity of the Confederate fire was evident in the numerous casualties suffered during the advance and retreat.[276]

First Lieutenant Orson W. Bennett of Company A, 102nd U.S. Colored Troops, led a daring second attempt to retrieve three abandoned artillery pieces positioned dangerously close to Confederate lines, within 150 yards of the enemy and 100 yards beyond the Union lines. Selecting just thirty men for the task, Bennett ordered his men forward under heavy fire. Moving with precision and maintaining discipline, they were partially shielded by low brush and a slight rise in the terrain until they reached the guns, surrounded by fallen soldiers and horses. As the Confederates prepared to fire, Bennett commanded, "Down!" The men dropped to the ground, avoiding a deadly volley of grape and canister shot that passed over them. Rising quickly, they seized the first cannon and dragged it back to safety. Repeating this maneuver for the second and third guns, they worked under constant fire, narrowly avoiding Confederate attacks. Many who were wounded quite severely refused to go to the rear; they kept on fighting while the blood was flowing from their wounds.[277]

The Union troops cheered their successful retrieval, while Confederate forces shouted in frustration. That evening, the 102nd, along with the 127th New York, held the front to cover the Union retreat. It was also assigned the task of transporting wounded soldiers three miles to the nearest landing. The men's courage at Honey Hill, despite the loss of two men and eighteen wounded, earned them respect from white troops for their bravery and determination in a challenging fight. Following the engagement, Chaplain William Waring wrote, "The '102d' has won for itself a proud name.…You can tell the ladies of Detroit that the flag they gave us waves over none but brave and determined soldiers." Colonel Chipman is a "brick, there being no fear in that man; always as cool as a cucumber," adding in another letter,

"On one side of our little detail of 300 men the 54th Massachusetts (colored) was drawn up, on the other side a white regiment, the 127th New York. Here our forced sustained a charge from the enemy and charged in turn. In this affair the 102nd covered themselves in glory. It is acknowledged without stint on all hands that our regiment maintained the steadfast line of battle and fought with the greatest determination of any troops on the ground."[278]

Years later, Lieutenant Bennett was awarded the Medal of Honor for his actions at Honey Hill, and the entire 102nd received great praise for its actions during the battle. An unnamed correspondent, who was most likely an officer with the regiment, wrote about the battle, "In this affair the 102nd covered themselves in glory. It is acknowledged without a stint on all hands that our regiment maintained the steadfast line of battle and fought with the greatest determination of any troops on the ground." After rescuing the cannons, the 102nd moved to Bull's Neck, where it was likewise engaged. The same correspondent praised the men's actions in this location as well:

> *Here again they had several skirmishes and one severe fight, where the 102d fought as well as any troops ever fought, no other Michigan regiment excepted. There were men in my company who were shot through and through the fleshy part of the arm who have not gone to hospital, but after having their wounds dressed have come to their company quarters, remained there, and seemed scarcely to notice their wounds. If such a thing had occurred in the regiment I formerly belonged to, such a wound would have been good for a three-months' stay in some hospital at Philadelphia or Baltimore. There are others who are wounded in the neck and side, but have full use of their limbs, who would go back to the field at once if they were permitted to do so. The same is true of every company of the regiment. Now such bravery I never saw before. I have known men to fight as well and bravely as men ever fought, but never before have I known men to fight on after being severely wounded, and anxious to return to the field of battle as soon as their wounds were dressed. After having been three and a half years in the field and participated in sixteen different engagements, I never before saw men exhibit such unyielding bravery in battle.*

Honey Hill marked the beginning of a series of intense engagements with Confederate forces for the 102nd U.S. Colored Troops. On the morning of December 7, 1864, the regiment joined the famed 54th Massachusetts in the Battle of Tulifinny, where the Union's objective was to destroy the strategically crucial Tulifinny Bridge, a key part of the Confederate supply line. Alerted by their pickets, Confederate forces mobilized, organizing quickly at the bridge and advancing on the Union troops. Positioned south and west of the bridge, Confederate soldiers launched a fierce counterattack, nearly overwhelming the Union forces as they arrived. Forced to fall back, the Confederates then fortified their position along the railroad line as rain poured down, worsening conditions for both sides.[279]

On a cold, wet December 9, Union forces, including the 102nd, made one final attempt to break the Confederate line. At 8:45 a.m., ten Union artillery pieces unleashed a barrage to clear the way for the advancing troops. As the fighting continued, the Confederate forces made a fierce movement, their mobbish "Rebel yell" echoing through the woods as they hoped to push the Union lines, only to be met by determined Union lead. With ammunition dwindling on both sides, the Union forces eventually decided to withdraw, executing a slow, controlled retreat to the fortified position at Deveaux's Neck. This well-coordinated fallback prevented a serious Confederate counterattack, as the Confederates themselves faced a shortage of ammunition. Following this engagement, the 102nd spent the rest of the month active doing picket and fatigue duty and fierce patrols in the region. In most of these engagements, they participated as detachments, where several companies of the regiment were present. Rarely did the 102nd fight as a unified regiment.[280]

Chapter 18

1865

Marching Toward Liberation

Chaplain William Waring of the 102nd USCT provided a striking, detailed account of Sherman's army entering Beaufort early in 1865. He encouraged readers to "stand upon the sidewalk and notice them as they pass along." His descriptions began with the sight of a soldier, his pants torn "halfway up to his knee," with "unshaven" face and "unshorn" hair, wearing a hat with its crown missing. This soldier marched "perfectly oblivious to the eyes that are upon him, or the remarks that are made about him." With his gun swung over his shoulder, his entire demeanor conveyed confidence; "the whole appearance of the man says, 'I can hold all the ground that I cover.'" Waring likened this type to frontiersmen in the western wilds, explaining, "You have seen the same character in the Western wilds, bent on capturing some fine old buck," except now, Waring wrote, "he is after a Johnny."[281]

Waring's observations continued, remarking on another soldier who took pride in his unique dress, not wearing "a regulation hat or an army cap, but an old fashioned helmet with a prodigious horse tail streaming down his back." This soldier, Waring noted, felt "particularly glorious that he has contributed so much in overthrowing the doctrine that soldiers should be dressed in uniform." But the scene was not without darker moments. Waring described incidents revealing the "negro-hating element." He described how "one of them takes a colored woman's pies and then slaps her over because she complained," and another soldier "inflicts a wound on an already wounded colored soldier." Hostility even reached the quarters of the post band, which was composed of Black musicians. Two soldiers entered and tried to cause trouble but were met with an unexpected response: "One of the bandsmen unceremoniously knocks them down stairs."[282]

Waring also recorded contrasting moments of warmth and humor in the soldiers' interactions with the Black community. He recounted a soldier "full of fun," who encountered an "old contraband lady of fresh arrival." Instead of harassment, this soldier threw his arms around her, exclaiming with joy, "Hurrah, old woman, bully for you!"[283]

On January 19, 1865, several companies of the 102nd returned from outpost duty to their base camp in Beaufort. Just days later, on January 22, the regiment departed Beaufort aboard a steamer, traveling upriver to Boyd's Neck, and then established camp at Deveaux's Neck. There, on January 24, they regrouped with a detachment that had been operating with Foster's brigade. By January 28, the regiment had advanced to Pocotaligo, where it constructed rifle pit fortifications to withstand the cold. Many soldiers built small shanties with fireplaces to keep warm as they moved north toward Charleston. After crossing the Salkehatchie River, the 102nd encountered Confederate forces at Cuckold Creek on February 9, with Companies B, E and I engaging in a skirmish against Rebel cavalry. Under Confederate artillery fire, the regiment fell back three miles and set up camp for the night.[284]

The regiment then continued its mission, dismantling railroad tracks and constructing breastworks near Cuckold Creek, where it remained until February 14. From there, the men marched to the Ashepoo River, building a bridge across it and advancing toward Charleston. They reached the Ashley River on February 23 but found the bridge destroyed, preventing their crossing. Finally, on February 27, they secured boats to cross the river and moved toward Charleston's defenses at Charleston Neck, located in the rear of the city. The lieutenant, leading his company, recounted orders to destroy everything in their path, including a strategic railroad bridge over the Santee River connecting Savannah to Charleston. Some soldiers, likely newer recruits, made this long march barefoot due to lack of issued footwear or worn-out shoes. In an exhausting effort, they demolished the drawbridge and tore up a mile of railroad through the marshlands.[285]

As they advanced, the regiment set fire to homes and other structures to prevent Confederate forces from using them, suffering casualties along the way. Among the fallen was Quartermaster Patrick McLaughlin of Detroit, who was killed and robbed of his personal belongings; his body was later recovered and sent back to his family. The 102nd pressed on, dismantling the railroad until reaching Charleston. With Confederate forces recently evacuated, the 102nd became one of the first regiment to march triumphantly into the city.[286]

After spending a few days at Charleston Neck, the 102nd was ordered to Savannah, Georgia. Upon making its way out of South Carolina, it was discovered that there was not enough transports to take the entire regiment. Due to this, the regiment would unfortunately be split up once again; only the left wing was able to make its way down the coast, under arriving in Savannah the following day on March 8. The right wing would arrive days later on the eleventh. Now in Savanah, the regiment marched through the city to its rear, where it found shanties to camp in that were previously used by Sherman's army, and brigaded with the noble 54th and 55th Massachusetts. In the area, the regiment did fatigue duty, which included burying dead horses, which Captain Nelson noted was "not a very pleasant occupation."[287]

In his letters, Dr. Curtis offered vivid snapshots of Savannah, capturing the city's allure as well as its tensions. He described his first impressions: "This is a most beautiful city. It looks like home, after being in such a hole as Charleston. The city is built on a high bluff; the streets are clean, buildings are in good condition, and the streets are lined with shade trees. The city has large numbers of parks, and in these are monuments, among which I saw the Pulaski Monument! We are encamped just out of town on good high ground." Settling into camp life, he added a humble description of his quarters: "You will find Dr. S. & myself in a board shanty, double roof, about 12 x 14 feet, two windows, a fireplace, tables, [and] marble mantelpiece."[288]

But Curtis's observations extended beyond Savannah's aesthetics to its social complexities, particularly as he noted the interactions between Black soldiers and the mixed-race women of the South: "As my eye wanders down little streets in the camp, I see the boys in their Sunday rig, collected in little squads here & there, conversing with the colored ladies of Savannah." He was struck by the beauty and diversity of these women, "from the jet-black wench to the white girl who by her features & complexion proves her to be the offspring of some aristocratic father by a slave mother." These women, embodying "the blood of the most noble families," existed on the fringes of both Black and white communities, belonging fully to neither. "But think of the curse—they are neither companion for the white or black. The curse of caste on the one side & on the other, they are called the mean White nigger &c."[289]

Although he found Savannah itself "a very fine town," Curtis was sharply aware of the hostility many residents, including Union soldiers, held toward Black troops. Reflecting on the prejudice around him, he observed, "We like Savannah very well, but it is one of the meanest of all kinds of people; the white soldiers are among the number. Many of our men get insult upon insult from the white soldiers, & these poor devils know just enough to let their own prejudice run away with their good sense." Yet the Black soldiers were not entirely defenseless, he noted, as some would stand up to this abuse by delivering "a good hammering."[290]

On Tuesday, March 28, marking one year since the regiment had departed Detroit, the unit was once again divided as it prepared to leave its camp in Savannah and embark for South Carolina. The next morning, the left wing—which consisted of Companies E, B, A, G and K—boarded the steamship *Planter* and officially departed Georgia. This famed vessel carried its own remarkable history: just a few years prior, Robert Smalls (1839–1915), an enslaved crew member on the Confederate steamer, made history on the ship. With the white officers ashore, Smalls and his Black crew took control of the ship, navigating it through Charleston Harbor past Confederate defenses, including Fort Sumter. Successfully reaching the Union's Atlantic Blockading Squadron, Smalls and his crew secured their freedom and delivered valuable intelligence to Union forces.[291]

The left wing of the 102nd traveled up the coast to Hilton Head, stopping briefly in Beaufort before continuing to Georgetown, South Carolina, north of Charleston, where it arrived on April 1. In this town, Dr. Curtis described the contrabands he encountered, noting their ragged, patched clothing, which displayed "all the colors of the rainbow" and ranged from broadcloth to calico, even corn sacks. Their pants varied just as widely, with some fashioned from materials like satin and Brussels carpeting, creating a vivid and mismatched appearance. Curtis observed that many had gone without shoes so long that their feet had hardened and cracked, resembling "the hide of an elephant." The formerly enslaved people spoke of their harsh conditions, explaining that their annual rations were limited to twelve bushels of corn, a single pair of shoes and twelve yards of coarse cloth. Any additional food was scarce, and occasionally they would receive a small piece of bacon, but usually they had to resort to stealing to supplement their diet. Curtis remarked that they now felt as though their "day of jubilee" had come, hopeful in their newfound freedom.[292]

As the regiment was divided into two wings, it's challenging to cover their actions simultaneously. The next two chapters will therefore detail each wing's expeditions separately.

Chapter 19

Chipman's Fierce Right Wing

The right wing of the 102nd United States Colored Troops, led by Colonel Chipman and consisting of Companies C, D, F, H and I, began its movement from Georgia to Charleston in early April. On April 7, it received orders to embark for Charleston and boarded the ship around ten o'clock that evening. The following day, April 8, it set sail at sunrise and arrived in Beaufort by noon. Resuming its journey at sunrise on April 9, it reached Charleston by midday. Upon disembarking, the troops returned to their previous camp on Charleston Neck. Soon after, they were ordered to prepare for an expedition up the Santee River to join General Potter's forces. This mission was a formidable challenge, as the men were aware that the rural area they would traverse was heavily patrolled by Confederate cavalry.[293]

At 7:00 a.m. on the morning of April 11, the right wing made its way out of camp, traveling about sixteen miles north by rail before continuing the journey on foot. While en route on the expedition, Lieutenant William E. Sleight and Company D of the 102nd U.S. Colored Troops were halted on their march during this expedition, taking a brief moment to rest and make coffee. "We were at ease, unaware of any immediate threat," Sleight later recorded, "when suddenly, out of the nearby woods, a squad of rebel cavalry sneaked upon us, unleashing a volley of gunfire." Although only one soldier was wounded, the ambush was a stark reminder of the dangers they faced. Quickly, the men sprang into action, forming a skirmish line with squads stationed at the flanks, front and rear. Sleight was assigned to guard the left side, where they soon encountered "several skirmishes that afternoon with the rebels, though thankfully, none were wounded."[294]

As night fell, the right wing reached the Santee River, expecting to board a gunboat to transport it five miles upstream. "But upon reaching the landing, the boat was nowhere in sight," Sleight noted, weariness creeping into his words. Forced to wait, the company set up picket duty, with Sleight and his men stationed half a mile from the main camp. Throughout the night, the distant sounds of Confederate artillery and cavalry movements kept the men on edge, expecting an attack that never came.[295]

By noon the next day, the gunboat finally arrived, and the regiment began to move. But as Sleight withdrew his pickets, Confederate forces sensed their movement and bore down on his position. "My men would have to cross a creek on the bare stringers of a bridge the rebels had destroyed, a perfect trap if they caught us mid-crossing," he recounted. Thinking quickly, Sleight commanded the orderly sergeant to keep ten of the best men behind in the dense underbrush as a defensive line. When the main group began crossing, the Rebel cavalry charged down the road, firing wildly. Sleight and his men in the underbrush opened fire, "dropping several of them from their saddles." The sudden attack caused the Confederate troops to scatter, giving Sleight's group time to safely retreat to the gunboat, where the rest of the right wing was boarding.[296]

In the afternoon of April 15, the gunboat set off up the Santee River, carrying a heavy load of soldiers. As they neared a high bluff, tension filled the air. "The gunboat commander warned me that the rebels would likely lie in wait at the bluff, and that, overloaded as we were, we couldn't use the boat's naval guns," Sleight wrote. He quickly positioned his men along the railing of the bow, organizing them into two ranks: "The first knelt, muskets ready, while the second stood behind, prepared to fire." As they rounded a sharp bend, Confederate forces appeared on the bluff, taking aim at the boat. "Open fire!" Sleight commanded, and the river erupted in gunfire. Confederate bullets rained down, battering the boat's steel-plated pilothouse, while the men held steady under Sleight's leadership. The exchange lasted half an hour, with dense smoke from the exchange clouding the view. Once they passed out of range, the boat commander confirmed their success. "From the pilot house, he saw the effect of our fire and said we'd killed and wounded many of them," Sleight wrote.[297]

Exhausted, the regiment disembarked as night fell, setting up camp along the riverbank. Just as Sleight began to relax, an orderly arrived with orders to report to Colonel Chipman. "I was startled," he admitted, knowing that he had disobeyed Chipman's command not to fire the first shot. In the colonel's tent, Chipman looked him over and asked simply, "Lieutenant, who fired the first shot?" Sleight responded without hesitation, "I did, Sir." Chipman replied, "That's all," leaving Sleight with lingering uncertainty about the consequences. However, other officers, aware of Sleight's quick decision to prevent disaster, quietly assured him of their support.[298]

On April 17, the regiment resumed its march to join General Potter's forces, approximately forty to fifty miles away. Acting as rear guard, Sleight led his company cautiously through enemy territory. Around noon, a formerly enslaved local informed Colonel Chipman that Confederate cavalry lay in ambush along the road. The informant pointed out a hidden byroad, allowing the regiment to avoid the trap. Taking the route, they advanced cautiously and finally camped on a wooded hill that night, with Sleight's company on high alert as pickets.[299]

The following morning, on April 18, 1864, Sleight's men took the lead. "I made sure every musket was loaded, bayonets fixed," he wrote, knowing that they were close to another confrontation. Only a short way down the road, Confederate pickets fired. "We spread out as skirmishers and charged forward," Sleight recounted, pressing the Rebels back into an open field where they had constructed a barricade. Outnumbered, Sleight sent a runner to Chipman, who quickly sent reinforcements. "We flanked them on the left and drove them out, suffering only minor casualties," Sleight reported. As they continued forward, the regiment neared a swamp where the only crossing was a narrow, waterlogged path completely covered by Confederate artillery. The enemy had positioned two twenty-four-pound cannons on the far side, prepared for an ambush. As the regiment began crossing, Rebel forces attacked from behind, forcing Sleight's company to engage in defensive maneuvers.[300]

In a stroke of luck, Lieutenant Barrell, sent the previous night to request reinforcements, returned with forty Union cavalrymen just as the regiment approached the Confederate battery. "Barrell's timing was miraculous," Sleight wrote, recognizing that the capture of the guns likely saved his company from a deadly trap. With the battery neutralized, the regiment crossed safely and advanced without further resistance. During Barrell's mission, he came upon a Confederate officer and orderly. He captured the orderly and forced him to direct him through the Confederate lines, which allowed him to achieve his mission that helped the right wing. In 1891, the Medal of Honor was awarded to Barrell for this action. The citation simply reads, "Hazardous service in marching through the enemy's country to bring relief to his command."[301]

The wing finally reached General Potter on the night of April 19, marching many days and miles through enemy territory with only five companies. The troops faced the constant threat of attack by larger forces and the risk of being isolated without reinforcements, all while enduring severe hardship and exhaustion. Their successful arrival was a testament to the resilience and determination of the troops.[302]

Chapter 20

Clark's Left Wing

The left wing marched out of Georgetown, South Carolina, at eight o'clock in the morning on April 5, 1865, commanded by Major Clark, on an expedition commonly known as "Potter's Raid" under command of General Potter's Provisional Division. It included the 1st Brigade, commanded by Colonel Philip P. Brown of the 157th New York, along with detachments from the 56th New York and the 25th and 107th Ohio. The 2nd Brigade, led by Colonel Hallowell, consisted of the 54th Massachusetts, eight companies of the 32nd United States Colored Troops and five companies of the 102nd United States Colored Troops (left wing). Additionally, there were detachments from the 1st New York Engineers and the 4th Massachusetts Cavalry and two cannons from Battery B of the 3rd New York Artillery, totaling around 2,500 men. Before their departure, General Quincy Adams Gillmore conducted a review of the force in a large plowed field.[303]

The 102nd began its march through a dense forest, covering nineteen miles without encountering Confederate forces. At nightfall, the men camped near Johnson's Swamp, with soldiers reflecting on the journey ahead and the unknown challenges they would face in the days to come. On April 6, the regiment moved into more favorable terrain of rolling hills, which allowed foraging parties to gather supplies and secure draft animals. After another nineteen miles, they set up camp near Thorntree Swamp, with Kingstree lying seven miles away across the Black River. The abundance of resources renewed the soldiers' strength and heightened their resolve.[304]

Setting out early on April 7, the column moved northwest, passing through open countryside with more provisions available. Foragers gathered supplies, but in compliance with orders, they also destroyed cotton fields and mills to weaken the Confederacy's economic infrastructure. Reaching the Northeastern Railroad, the troops tore up miles of track, preventing Confederate movement. The 102nd received orders to destroy the Kingstree Bridge over the Black River, and after a brief exchange of fire with a small Confederate force, they succeeded, effectively severing a key transportation route. The next day, on April 8, the column marched along fair roads under clear skies, occasionally spotting Confederate scouts on the flanks. Their path led westward, but a false report of a destroyed bridge ahead forced them to detour. After covering eighteen miles, they made camp near Manning, their anticipation of an enemy encounter growing stronger with each passing day.[305]

In the early hours of April 9, at 1:30 a.m., the men broke camp and crossed the Pocotaligo Bridge under darkness. By dawn, a light rain began to fall as they advanced toward Sumterville, passing through plantations where hundreds of colored individuals followed the brigade. Confederate troops offered light resistance but fell back quickly. Intelligence indicated that Confederate forces were entrenched at Dingle's Mill on Turkey Creek, about four miles from Sumterville, with a force of five hundred men, mostly militia, and three artillery pieces. As the division halted one mile from the mill, a flanking maneuver by Hallowell's brigade was attempted; an inexperienced guide led them astray, and they returned as the main force engaged the Confederates directly. After a brief but intense engagement, the Union troops broke through, and the 102nd marched into Sumterville by nightfall, securing the town and its resources.[306]

On April 10, the 102nd resumed its mission of dismantling Confederate infrastructure. Near Manchester, they set fire to a covered bridge, burned four railcars, destroyed two hundred bales of cotton and leveled a gin house and a corn mill. The regiment also rendered three locomotives and fifteen railcars useless, ensuring that nothing of value remained. Their work served as a significant blow to the Confederate supply network and a testament to the Union's resolve. The next day, April 11, they advanced twelve miles toward Manchester. The 102nd and its fellow regiments pressed forward, driven by the mission's successes and the mounting sight of colored men and women adding to the rear of the line following behind the expedition. A few days later, the regiment faced Confederate forces once again on a rainy April 15 near Spring Hill.[307]

On April 18, 1865, General Potter's Union forces, including the 102nd United States Colored Troops, advanced from Camden toward Stateburg,

South Carolina. Moving along the main road with minimal resistance, Potter's troops encountered a fortified Confederate position at Swift Creek. General Pierce M.B. Young led the Confederate defense, which included four hundred men from Lewis's Tennessee brigade, 350 mounted troops from Hannon's Alabama brigade and Hamilton's field artillery battery.[308]

Potter devised a right flanking maneuver to outwit the entrenched defenders. While his main body demonstrated along the creek, he sent the 54th Massachusetts, the 102nd USCT and the 107th Ohio Infantry to attempt a crossing farther down the stream, guided by a local resident. Lieutenant Colonel Hooper led the 54th through muddy, ploughed fields along the swamp's edge, with Captain Bridge's Company F providing skirmish support. Local informants alerted the Union forces that the swamp was only passable two miles down at Boykin's Mills, where the creek had been dammed.[309]

As the Union troops approached Boykin's Mills, they spotted Confederate scouts retreating. Captain Bridge advanced his skirmishers along the road toward the mills, eventually revealing a dammed pond created by a dike with sluice gates at each end. Recognizing an opportunity, the Union command ordered the 54th to cross the narrow dike in single file, aiming to establish a foothold on the far bank despite the challenging, exposed approach. Under the leadership of Lieutenant Reed, the men of the 54th bravely charged across the dike under fire, with Corporal William H. Brown of Company K notably leading the way and earning distinction for his courage.[310]

After a fierce skirmish, the Confederate forces fell back, allowing the Union troops to secure the position around 4:00 p.m. The victory was heralded by cheers as the 102nd USCT, the 107th Ohio and troops along the main road pressed forward, driving the Confederates into retreat. Leaving Boykin's Mills, the 54th Massachusetts reunited with the main division, and the Union troops marched several more miles before camping for the night, exhausted but victorious. Colonel Henry L. Chipman soon joined the encampment with the right wing of the 102nd USCT, completing their journey to find General Potter and rendezvous with the rest of their regiment. A thunderstorm erupted that evening, drenching the soldiers as they prepared for the next day's challenges, marking another night of dedication and perseverance in the expedition.[311]

Chapter 21

The Last Push for Freedom

Lieutenant William E. Sleight described the poignant and chaotic days as the right wing closed in on its destination, accompanied by a thousands of contrabands who had followed the Union army's march in pursuit of freedom. These individuals, ranging from young children to the very elderly, carried with them the few belongings they could gather such as old blankets, tattered rags, cornmeal and bacon. Many appeared frail, as though they had endured a lifetime of hardship under slavery, some seeming close to one hundred years old. They shuffled along with determination, struggling to keep up with the troops. This procession was a powerful image of freedom's first, tentative steps, as people burdened by both physical exhaustion and the weight of the unknown future sought security in the shadow of the Union army. The soldiers, now surrounded by these former slaves, witnessed firsthand the costs of emancipation and the resilience of people finally stepping away from bondage.[312]

As Sleight's regiment encountered Confederate resistance, skirmishes broke out, causing many of the contrabands to scatter in search of shelter. The threat of combat made the freedpeople's journey even more perilous, underscoring their vulnerability even in freedom's pursuit. While on their march, the news of Lee's surrender arrived, bringing relief and celebration among soldiers and freedpeople alike. They fired their muskets in symbolic recognition of peace. But this sense of victory was painfully short-lived. As they approached Georgetown, South Carolina, the devastating news of President Lincoln's assassination reached them, casting a profound sadness over the troops. For the soldiers and contrabands, Lincoln represented hope for a new life, and his death was a stark reminder that the path to true freedom would be long and fraught with challenges. The army's joy turned to mourning, and the sense of a triumphant end to the war was tempered by the somber reality of rebuilding and securing freedom in the wake of such a profound loss.[313]

At dawn on April 19, the 102nd, now as a full force with the brigade, resumed its advance. Confederate forces attempted to halt their progress with makeshift rail breastworks and artillery, but Union regiments, including the 25th Ohio and the 157th New York, drove them back. The 102nd executed another flanking maneuver with the 32nd USCT and the 107th Ohio, forcing the Confederates across Big Rafting Creek and securing a key victory. On April 20, the regiment reached Middleton Depot, where Potter's forces focused on demolishing Confederate resources. For two miles, Union troops burned 16 locomotives, 245 railcars and massive stores of ordnance and supplies, which exploded in deafening blasts. By the end of the day, these important pieces of Confederate infrastructure had been obliterated, a testament to the determination and discipline of the Union forces.[314]

With orders to return to Georgetown, the 102nd began its journey back on April 21. Early in the morning, about two hundred Confederates attacked Company A of the 102nd on picket duty, but the troops held their ground, repelling the attack and showcasing their resilience. Potter's Raid lasted twenty-one days, covering a grueling three hundred miles. Along the way, the 102nd and other Union regiments liberated thousands of formerly enslaved individuals who followed the troops to Georgetown. The raid's destruction of Confederate supplies and infrastructure dealt a severe blow to the Southern war effort. For the 102nd United States Colored Troops, this journey stood as a monumental testament to their courage, resilience and unwavering commitment to freedom, marking their place in history as liberators and defenders of a Union that they helped to preserve.[315]

Upon receiving news of the end of hostilities through a flag of truce, the 102nd was assigned to guard duty across various locations in South Carolina, marking the end of their combat service. By mid-May 1865, the regiment was stationed on occupation duty in Summerville, Branchville, Orangeburg and Winnsboro, South Carolina.[316]

On the twenty-ninth, the regiment received orders to proceed to Charleston, and the next day it embarked on transports, arriving the same day and establishing camp on Charleston Neck, where it remained until May 8. It then broke camp and marched for Summerville, reaching there and encamping until the nineteenth. Then it proceeded by rail to Branchville and thence on the twenty-fifth to Orangeburg, where it was engaged on provost guard and fatigue duty until July 28, after which it marched for Winnsboro, arriving there at the beginning of August. During the remainder of that month, it was engaged in fatigue duties in these areas. While traveling through Columbia, South Carolina, a soldier noted that it had been a very pleasant city once, but about half of the town was burned and lay in ruins.[317]

With the war essentially over, the men of the regiment found themselves quite bored in camp when not out doing fatigue duty. However, games like chess, which the men greatly enjoyed, helped to pass time. Dr. Curtis wrote that "soldiers are inclined to feel dull & lonely when encamped for a long time in one place," as they faced the same monotonous routine day after day. Now that peace had settled over the land, they had little to occupy their time but to recount "over & over the little incidents we are knowing to that have transpired during the past two or three years." Without night alarms, picket duty, skirmishing or the "wild & exciting duty" of foraging, their meals were meager unless they purchased additional goods. "So you see," Dr. Curtis continued, "we sit in camp and yarn it from morning, wishing ourselves at home perhaps a hundred times a day."[318]

In letters from Dr. Curtis and Lieutenant William E. Sleight of the 102nd USCT, a harrowing story emerges from June 16 in Orangeburg, South Carolina. On that day, an enslaved young man, about eighteen years old, escaped to the Union camp seeking freedom from his cruel bondage. Dr. Curtis described how the boy arrived early in the morning, burdened with a heavy two-inch chain locked around his neck with a large padlock. The chain ran down his body, beneath his clothing, and was similarly fastened around his ankle. This "ornament," as Curtis called it, had been forced on him since just before Christmas, causing painful callouses and raw sores where the metal had cut into his skin. Remarkably, the young man had marched twenty-five miles overnight with these chains to reach the Union lines.[319]

Lieutenant Sleight recalled the boy coming to his tent, pleading, "Master, would you please take this chain off of my neck, dat my Master put on long ago?" Examining the chain, Sleight found it to be an old-fashioned, long-linked train chain, running from the boy's neck to his ankle. After unlocking and removing it, Sleight noted the "thankful look" the boy gave him. When asked why his master had chained him, the young man replied, "'Cause I tried to run away to you Yankees."[320]

The provost marshal took the boy into care, and his former master was summoned to account for the brutal treatment of a "free man."

Reflecting on the encounter, Dr. Curtis denounced the "divine institution of Slavery," remarking that he had witnessed "instruments of torture that far go beyond this in barbarity." This story of endurance and liberation highlights both the suffering endured under slavery and the sense of relief and gratitude the young man felt upon reaching Union forces on that June day in Orangeburg.[321]

While in Summerville, South Carolina, Dr. Curtis described the regiment's mission to "advance into the country & garrison the towns in order to preserve peace." He observed that former Confederate soldiers were "comeing in by hundreds to Charleston taking the Oath of Allegiance & then...return to their homes," where they now treated Union soldiers "kindly & own up that they are whipped with very good grace." Dr. Curtis remarked on the interactions between locals and Black soldiers, noting that Southerners "mingle freely with our boys," with "some surprised to find that colored Soldiers are human beings."[322]

In another letter, Dr. Curtis reflected on the regiment's intense emotions after the assassination of President Lincoln, expressing that "it is a good thing the war closed when it did." He explained that if the conflict had continued, the soldiers would have waged "a war of utter extermination," as "many a man swore to avenge the honored President." Soldiers and officers, even those previously opposed to property destruction, vowed to "make a desert of the country" if the war persisted. Dr. Curtis noted that the soldiers' anger was so strong that local Confederates avoided them "until they were more calm." He attributed the end of hostilities to a "providential hand" that "interposed in time to save the lives of thousands of innocent beings."[323]

He also recounted an incident aboard a government transport where a Confederate refugee expressed doubt over Lincoln's death. An officer from the 102nd, overhearing her, sternly warned, "Madam were you a man I would throw you overboard," causing her to fall silent for the rest of the journey. Dr. Curtis underscored the profound grief and outrage felt by the Black soldiers, who "swore by high heaven to avenge Father Lincoln."[324]

On September 14, the regiment arrived in Charleston. After some time spent in the area, with many of the officers working hard to finish their muster-out rolls, the 102nd United States Colored Troops was officially mustered out of service on September 30. The regiment began its way back to the Wolverine State on October 3, divided in two separate wings. The journey home for Michigan's colored regiment began with a memorable visit to Fort Sumter and Morris Island on October 3, 1865. This stop held deep significance, as Fort Sumter marked the location where the Civil

War had erupted four years earlier, eventually leading to the loss of nearly 750,000 lives. Over the following days, the men spent time in Charleston, participating in a dress parade and drills.[325]

On October 9, they boarded the steamer *Edward Everett* but did not set sail until the next day. The voyage north was generally smooth, although a heavy gale on October 12 forced them to shelter in a Delaware breakwater. By October 13, they had reached New York Harbor, where they disembarked on October 14, crossed to Jersey City and boarded a train for the west. Their rail journey took them through Elmira and Hornellsville on October 15, with a stop in Dunkirk and breakfast in Erie, Pennsylvania, the next morning.[326]

After dinner in Cleveland, about five companies boarded the steamer *Cleveland City*, arriving at Detroit on October 17. They were treated to a hearty breakfast at the Michigan Central Depot. The *Free Press* acknowledged that the regiment "was received in about the same manner as a white regiment." It noted further, "They were congratulated by a large delegation of young women who followed them through the streets toward the barracks, waving colored handkerchiefs in unison with those of their admirers." In a rare moment of praise, the article concluded, "The colored troops fought nobly." A few days later, on the twentieth, the remaining five companies of the regiment returned to Detroit. Their travel aboard the steamship *City of Cleveland* was delayed due to heavy storms. The recent devastating fire at the freight depot prevented them from receiving the typical ceremonies held there, but the remaining companies were still treated to a warm welcome home with a hot dinner prepared for them at the barracks.[327]

Finally reunited with loved ones, the men of the 102nd United States Colored Troops could celebrate the end of a long and challenging chapter in their lives. Their return marked not only the joy of homecoming but also the honor of having served courageously in one of the Michigan's most significant regiments. Through their dedication, they had proven their bravery on the battlefield, earning respect and admiration. Now, as they rejoined their communities, they carried with them a legacy of strength and sacrifice that would forever be remembered in Michigan's history.[328]

In his memoir, Lieutenant Sleight reflected on his dedicated military service:

> *Thus ended a long term of four years and seven months in active service, nearly two of which I served as a commissioned officer in a Colored Regiment. Although some people have said to me, "You only*

had a commission in a nigger regiment," I was not—and am not—ashamed to have anyone know that I held a commission in what they call a "nigger regiment."

In the first place, every officer in this United States Colored Regiment had to pass an examination before a Board of Regular Army Officers to receive a commission, and they had to be men who had seen active service in the field. Moreover, they had to have grit to accept a position in one of these regiments because Confederate President Jefferson Davis, when informed that our government was organizing Colored Troops and officering them with white officers, issued an order to his army to never show respect to these officers, but instead to shoot or hang every one taken prisoner. Consequently, the man who accepted a commission in one of these regiments knew his fate if captured. It was no place for cowards.

Our Colored Regiment fought as well in battle as any troops—always brave and ready to go wherever ordered—and no troops could have done more than they did.

This was a cruel war, forced upon the Northern people and directly against the Lord's wishes. The Lord designed this country to be a free land where people could become educated and enlightened, learn to distinguish good from evil, and advance His cause. But this war was forced upon the North to extend slavery and ignorance across the United States, aiming to completely block the Lord's plan for the betterment of the whole world. It was an honor to have had a hand in such a war. This was not a war for territory or to uphold a kingdom. I thank the Lord that I was granted the honor of assisting in putting down such ungodly principles, and that He has spared my life and health to this day, so I may witness the good results of that war. I enlisted as a private and served through all grades of promotion to Lieutenant. When mustered out, the Government offered me a Captain's commission in the regular army. However, I did not accept, as I was sick of war and military duty.[329]

Chapter 22

Brothers in Arms to Neighbors in Peace

After the conclusion of the war, some of the veterans of the 102nd returned to their former lives, while others who had enlisted after being freed from slavery had to build new lives. Despite the accomplishments of these men, some faced intense discrimination after the war. On July 4, 1866, the 102nd United States Colored Troops joined other Michigan regiments in a grand ceremony in Detroit. The regiments marched through the city in a parade before formally transferring their flags to the State of Michigan for safekeeping.[330] The 102nd USCT handed over three flags, including its presentation flag, along with its regimental and national flags, both now housed in the Michigan State Archives. Although the exact dates when the regiment received these flags are unknown, it was common for regiments to carry multiple flags. The national flag, a silk banner with thirty-five stars, likely accompanied the regiment through the war's final days. A black crepe ribbon, often used in Victorian mourning practices, is attached to the staff, probably added after President Abraham Lincoln's assassination on April 15, 1865, as a mark of respect.[331]

The silk regimental flag, though now fragmentary, once likely displayed the U.S. coat of arms with thirty-five stars, representing the inclusion of West Virginia in the Union. Details about the flag's origin and use remain unknown. Two of the regiment's three flags have undergone conservation, carefully humidified and stabilized between layers of dyed netting to preserve their fragile silk. These historic flags, preserved by the State of Michigan, belong to the people of Michigan and are available for viewing by appointment through the state capitol staff.[332]

To tell the story of the 102nd United States Colored Troops without the tragic story of one of their own, John Taylor, would be incomplete. Just a year after the Civil War, Taylor's life, marked by resilience and sacrifice, took a devastating turn. Undoubtedly, one of Michigan's most overlooked and haunting stories lies in the shadows of its history, remaining largely untold and shrouded in darkness. Born into slavery in Kentucky, Taylor found his first taste of freedom when he encountered the Union army and became a servant to a chaplain from Hillsdale, Michigan. Coming to Michigan, he found himself in Jackson County, where in August 1864 Taylor enlisted in the 1st Michigan Colored Infantry at seventeen. He survived the war and returned to Jackson, Michigan, under the direction of a guardian appointed by the army. The guardian was ordered to hold Taylor's $500 bounty until he turned twenty-one. Taylor eventually left his guardian and went to work for a farmer named John Buck. Arriving to the Buck home in his former soldier uniform and knapsack with a white felt hat, he then worked for him for more than a month. After quitting, Buck refused to pay Taylor's wages, and there was an argument. Rumors spread quickly through the area that Taylor had injured or killed one or multiple female members of the Buck family, and Taylor was arrested in Bath Township.[333]

Newspaper reports from the time are equally contradictory about the crime that led to his arrest. One thing about the situation that isn't under contention is what happened to Taylor. A few days later, on the evening of August 27, 1866, after his arrest, a mob of one to two hundred people armed with guns, swords and other items gathered in rage outside the Ingham County Jail in Mason. They demanded Sheriff Moody give them the keys to the jail, but he declined. After this, enraged further, they broke down the door to the jail with sledges and iron bars. They found Taylor shackled and handcuffed and sought the sheriff to obtain the keys to unlock his restraints. This request was flatly denied. They then threw the man into a wagon, transported him near the depot and placed a rope around his neck in preparation for hanging. He was given a brief opportunity to make any confession he might wish to share with Mr. Buck, who was present throughout the ordeal.[334]

Afterward, he was hanged and left there for more than an hour. Following this, his body was taken down, loaded into a wagon and transported for burial. It was reported that his body was buried along the "Hogsback" on the road to Mason. During the incident, the sheriff suffered considerable bruising from the mob's rough treatment. It remains uncertain where this matter ultimately led. Newspaper reports later indicated that all of Mr.

Signage for John Taylor Memorial Park on Cedar Street in Delta Township, Michigan. *Maurice Imhoff.*

Buck's relatives involved in the incident had survived and recovered. Despite indictments against five men, nobody was held accountable for the murder of Taylor. In 2018, when this story was rediscovered, Dead Man's Hill Park, a site long rumored to be the location of his burial, was renamed John Taylor Memorial Park, and a Michigan Historical Marker was placed on the site telling Taylor's story.[335]

Despite this discrimination, there were some advantages to being a Union veteran. Many of the men of the 102nd were involved in the Grand Army of the Republic (GAR), a Civil War veterans organization. This organization lobbied for veteran causes and legislation and provided a space for veterans to meet and talk about their experiences. Unlike many groups at the time, the GAR was an interracial organization, although there were some segregated posts. Men from the 102nd can be found of the rolls of several Michigan GAR posts. Men of the regiment, like their white counterparts, also participated in reunions and veteran parades. There were posts consisting entirely of colored men, as well as posts that were integrated.[336]

Post No. 341, one of 10 GAR posts in Cass County and 461 in Michigan, was established after the Civil War and named after Mathew Artis. Artis, from Calvin Township, Michigan, enlisted on October 7, 1863, at age twenty-seven and served as a private in Company B, 1st Michigan Volunteer Colored Troops (later the 102nd U.S. Colored Troops). He died of disease on April 10, 1864, in Detroit. Post No. 341 was a Black GAR post with thirty-six members, including about twenty-one veterans of the 102nd USCT.[337]

Nineteen years after the 102nd U.S. Colored Troops disbanded, its first reunion was held on August 1, 1884, in Ann Arbor, commemorating the fiftieth anniversary of the emancipation of slaves in the West Indies. Seventy-four veterans of the 102nd USCT gathered with evident joy as they reminisced and shared memories of their service. The reunion began with a procession from the courthouse, led by the Toledo Cornet and Ann Arbor City Bands, down Main Street to Relief Park, where a large crowd enjoyed a midday meal. Between four and five thousand people gathered that afternoon for a literary program, which commenced at 2:00 p.m. on a platform adorned with distinguished guests, including President of the Day William Graves, Reverend John K. Hart, Reverend Samuel Haskell, Jerome A. Freeman, the Honorable Rufus Waples, Dr. T.P. Wilson and others.[338]

The program opened with a prayer by Reverend Hart, pastor of the African Methodist Episcopal Church in Ann Arbor, followed by a welcoming address from Mayor W.D. Harriman. Captain E.P. Allen of Ypsilanti responded with a brief yet heartfelt speech. J.H. Starks delivered a poem before introducing the keynote speaker, the Honorable James E. O'Hara, a Black congressman from North Carolina's second district. O'Hara's address traced the history of African people from their arrival in the West Indies to their struggles and victories, captivating the audience with his eloquent delivery. The Honorable A.J. Sawyer of Ann Arbor concluded the program with a brief but warmly received address. The day's celebrations culminated in an evening dance, making it a memorable occasion that honored the legacy of the 102nd USCT and celebrated the pride of the Black community.[339] Another was held in Dowagiac on August 1, 1891.[340]

The Michigan Soldiers' Home in Grand Rapids, established in 1885, provided a crucial haven for Civil War veterans in need, including Black soldiers who had served in the 102nd USCT. Intended as a residence for aging and disabled veterans, the home offered medical care, shelter and companionship for those who had endured the hardships of war and were without family support or sufficient resources in their later years. Several members of the 102nd USCT found respite here, underscoring Michigan's commitment to its Black veterans at a time when racial inequality was prevalent. According to Michigan's Grand Army of the Republic Memorial Hall and Museum archives, the Soldiers' Home embodied a commitment to honoring the sacrifices of Michigan's Civil War veterans, regardless of race, through essential postwar support and community.[341]

Writing fifty years after the war, Captain Wilbur Nelson noted:

> *I joined the black regiment on March 22, at Detroit, after two and a half years' service with a white regiment. The blacks made good soldiers, and were very proud of being soldiers, more so than white men. As soldiers they compared very favorably with the whites, although they put more dependence on the officers than did the white private soldiers. That is, a white soldier, in a pinch, would fight as well if there was no officer near to direct him, but it was different with the black soldier. The white soldiers came to form a good impression of them. As for bearing up under the hardships of a campaign, there was no perceptible difference between them and the whites.*[342]

Chapter 23

Preserving the Legacy of Freedom's Heroes

On June 9, 2021, Michigan State Representative Julie Alexander, joined by members of the Michigan Legislative Black Caucus, led a dedication of the day to honor the 102nd United States Colored Troops (USCT). With support from a state House vote, the day was officially recognized as "102nd United States Colored Troops Day" in Michigan. This designation aimed to raise awareness of the regiment's legacy and to pay tribute to the African American soldiers who fought courageously for the Union during the Civil War. The recognition by Michigan's legislature underscored the state's commitment to honoring the contributions of Black soldiers and increasing public understanding of their role in shaping both Michigan's and America's history.[343]

The unveiling and dedication of a State of Michigan historical marker for the 1st Michigan Colored Regiment on May 19, 1968, in Detroit was a significant event for Michigan's Black community and for the city's broader efforts to rebuild racial relations. Taking place at the former site of Camp Ward, where the regiment first assembled during the Civil War, the dedication honored the contributions of African American soldiers who had fought for freedom and justice more than a century prior. This event came at a time when Detroit was still healing from the devastating race riots of 1967, which had highlighted deep racial tensions and inequality. The marker not only recognized the historical significance of Michigan's Black soldiers but also symbolized the city's steps toward acknowledging African Americans' role in its history and future.[344]

The dedication ceremony, organized by the Association for the Study of Negro Life and History, was supported by prominent figures, including

State Representative Julie Alexander, of Hanover, speaks on the House floor in support of her resolution declaring June 9, 2021, to be 102nd United States Colored Troops Day in Michigan. *Michigan House Republicans.*

Detroit Mayor Jerome Cavanaugh and Michigan Governor George Romney. Both leaders spoke at the event, emphasizing the importance of unity and reconciliation. Mayor Cavanaugh, who had advocated for civil rights and urban renewal, used the occasion to highlight Detroit's commitment to healing racial divisions and building a more inclusive future. Governor Romney echoed these sentiments, recognizing the historical and contemporary struggles for equality faced by Michigan's African American communities. Their presence underscored the commitment of state and city leadership to honor Black history and to move forward with a renewed focus on racial justice.[345]

The marker dedication served as both a tribute to the past and a hopeful gesture toward future harmony. The event offered Detroit's Black community a sense of validation and pride in their historical contributions, while also providing the city's broader population with an opportunity for reflection and understanding. By commemorating the 1st Michigan Colored Regiment, the City of Detroit took a step toward acknowledging the sacrifices and achievements of African Americans, aiming to foster a climate of respect and shared history. This dedication helped set a tone for reconciliation in a

Members of the 102nd Colored Infantry Civil War reenactment group at Lansing's Mount Evergreen Cemetery in 1987: group founder Gerome Peebles (*center*), Smead Edwards (*left*), Fred Tittle (*kneeling*) and Melvin Poplar (*right*). *From the* Lansing State Journal.

city still scarred by the previous year's unrest, symbolizing a commitment to honoring diversity and building a more equitable society.[346]

History has traditionally been a tool for teaching values, with ancestors and heroes serving as role models for future generations. Unfortunately, African Americans were long presented with a narrow view of their heritage, often portrayed as mere victims until the end of slavery, with minimal recognition of their contributions to the nation's progress. In the 1800s, media coverage rarely celebrated African American heroism, instead reinforcing their victimhood—a perspective that has persisted, affecting self-esteem and expectations. This portrayal is not only inaccurate but also obscures the courage of African Americans who joined Abraham Lincoln's call, fighting for universal freedom in the armed forces.[347]

In the 1980s, as Civil War reenactments gained popularity in Michigan, these events were nearly all white, largely overlooking the pivotal role of African American soldiers from Michigan, like those in the 102nd United States Colored Troops. In 1986, William Peebles, a Marine Corps veteran

The John Taylor Historical Marker in Holt, Michigan, honors the memory of John Taylor, a Black resident who was lynched by a mob in 1866 after being accused of a crime without a fair trial. The marker, unveiled in November 2019, sheds light on this tragic event, acknowledging the injustice that Taylor faced and its impact on local history. *Maurice Imhoff.*

from Lansing with twenty-two years of service, including two tours in Vietnam, wanted to change that. That year, he founded the 102nd United States Colored Infantry Troops, a living history organization to bring the role of Black soldiers in the Civil War to life through reenactments, camp life demonstrations, military drills and memorials. Recognizing the untold contributions of African American men in the war, Peebles reportedly invested up to $40,000 of his own funds to outfit the group, and by 1998, it had grown to more than fifteen dedicated living historians.[348]

As the organization expanded, it formed into three companies: Company A in Lansing, Company B in Detroit and Company C in Flint. By 2024, two of these companies, Companies B and C, remained active. Operating primarily in mid-Michigan, Company C now comprises over twenty high school and college students who are committed to honoring the memory of the young men who fought for freedoms that benefit us today. These organizations speak for those who can no longer tell their stories, educating the public about the liberation of American slaves, the significance of the

Members of the 102nd USCT, Company C, reenactors, 2024. *David Sherman Begg.*

102nd USCT and the strength of faith that motivated them. Their mission is to portray these noble heroes as victors, not victims, celebrating their resilience and achievements as a source of inspiration and self-esteem for today's youth.[349]

In 2013, Michigan State Senator Coleman A. Young II introduced Senate Bill 93 to honor the 102nd United States Colored Troops. The bill designated a section of Interstate 375 within Wayne County as the "102nd United States Colored Troops (U.S.C.T.) Memorial Highway." This designation was enacted through Public Act 494 of 2014, becoming effective on March 31, 2015. The state legislature did not allocate funds for constructing two signs along I-375.[350]

In 2020, however, more than one hundred Michigan community members raised $3,200 to cover the cost of manufacturing and installing the signs. Due to the signs' location on the busy Detroit freeway, an on-site ceremony wasn't feasible. Instead, on Sunday, March 28, 2021—marking the 161st anniversary of the regiment's departure from Detroit—a dedication ceremony was held at the historical marker at the site of Camp Ward. The event saw a strong turnout, including reenactors from the 102nd USCT and soldiers from the Michigan National Guard. Among the speakers were former State Senator Coleman A. Young II and Lieutenant Governor Garlin Gilchrist, Detroit's

Former State Senator Coleman A. Young Jr. (*left*), with Maurice Imhoff (*right*) and Jaycob Sneed (*center*), for the unpacking of the soon-to-be-installed memorial highway sign. Photo taken in 2021. *Wayne Dabney*.

Photograph of Michigan Lieutenant Governor Garlin Gilchrist speaking at the 102nd USCT Memorial Highway sign dedication ceremony (*right*). Maurice Imhoff is standing in uniform (*left*). March 28, 2021. *Wayne Dabney.*

102nd USCT Memorial Highway sign on I-375 in Detroit, Michigan, 2021. *Maurice Imhoff.*

own and Michigan's first African American lieutenant governor. "The fact that this is a unit that was born here in Detroit, Michigan, is a pride for our entire state," remarked the lieutenant governor. The memorial highway serves as a tribute to the regiment's contributions and sacrifices during the Civil War, preserving their legacy in Michigan.[351]

Epilogue

As we close the pages of this history, it is essential to remember that the story of the 102nd United States Colored Troops is not merely one of battles fought and victories won, but of enduring courage, sacrifice and a relentless quest for freedom and justice. These men, many of whom were born into bondage or deep within the grips of systemic oppression, found themselves fighting not only for a country that had often failed to recognize their humanity but also for the ideals of equality and liberty. They marched into battle, knowing the risks yet driven by a sense of duty to liberate others still held in chains. Their actions on and off the battlefield laid the groundwork for future generations to inherit a more just and inclusive nation.

The legacy of Michigan's colored regiment is woven into the fabric of American history, as indelible as the scars left on the battlefield and the memories carried by those who survived. These soldiers were not just witnesses to a transformative era in our nation's history—they were themselves transformative agents. They carried forward a mission of hope, one that echoed the aspirations of all those who had been marginalized and oppressed. In the face of discrimination and daunting odds, they remained steadfast, embodying resilience and resolve in their journey to realize true freedom for all. Their lives and sacrifices continue to serve as a source of pride and inspiration, a testament to the power of unity and the unyielding pursuit of dignity and justice. This book stands as a tribute not only to the courage of those who served but also to the communities that supported

Artwork by Paul Collins. The child in the Michael Jordan "23" jersey symbolizes the gratitude we owe to the soldiers who fought for our liberty. *Paul Collins.*

them and the families who kept their memories alive, passing down stories of valor that deserve to be honored and remembered.

As we reflect on this chapter in history, let us acknowledge the struggles that these men faced even after the war, as many returned to find their lives threatened by prejudice and violence. The brutal lynching of John Taylor and the relentless discrimination experienced by other veterans of the regiment serve as stark reminders of the challenges that African American soldiers endured, both on the battlefield and back home. Their bravery was not simply in facing the Confederate forces but in confronting a society that continued to question their worth.

Today, as we stand on the foundation laid by these soldiers, we are called to continue their work, advancing the ideals of equality and freedom. They fought with the conviction that a brighter future was possible, even when that future seemed distant. Their legacy calls us to remember that the fight for justice is ongoing and that their sacrifices must inform our actions and commitments. In remembering the 1st Michigan Colored Regiment/102nd United States Colored Troops, we remember that history is not just about the past—it is a guide for the future. May this story inspire continued vigilance against oppression and a commitment to the vision of a free, equal and just society that these brave men held dear. Their fight lives on in us, and as long as we remember, they remain ever present in the American story.

Notes

Foreword

1. Mark E. Neely Jr., *The Civil War and the Limits of Destruction* (Harvard University Press, 2007).

Chapter 1

2. Earnest McBride, "African Americans in Michigan," *Michigan History Magazine* 84, no. 5 (2000): 28–33.
3. Jacqueline L. Tobin and Raymond G. Dobard, *Hidden in Plain View: The Secret Story of Quilts and the Underground Railroad* (Anchor Books, 1999).
4. David L. Lewis, *King: A Critical Biography* (University of Illinois Press, 2018).
5. Lewis Walker and Benjamin C. Wilson, *Michigan's Black Soldiers and the Civil War* (Michigan State University Press, 2001).
6. Lewis, *King*; McBride, "African Americans in Michigan."
7. James M. McPherson, *The Negro's Civil War: How American Blacks Felt and Acted During the War for the Union* (Vintage, 1991).
8. Ira Berlin et al., *Freedom's Soldiers: The Black Military Experience in the Civil War* (Cambridge University Press, 1998).
9. McPherson, *Negro's Civil War*.
10. Berlin et al., *Freedom's Soldiers*.

11. Eric Foner, *The Fiery Trial: Abraham Lincoln and American Slavery* (W.W. Norton & Company, 2010).
12. Berlin et al., *Freedom's Soldiers.*

Chapter 2

13. James M. McPherson, *Battle Cry of Freedom: The Civil War Era* (Oxford University Press, 1988).
14. Foner, *Fiery Trial.*
15. John David Smith, "Lincoln, the Emancipation Proclamation, and the Recruitment of Black Soldiers," *American Nineteenth Century History* 8, no. 2 (2007): 205–32.
16. McPherson, *Battle Cry of Freedom.*
17. Foner, *Fiery Trial.*
18. Norman McRae, *Negroes in Michigan During the Civil War* (Michigan Civil War Centennial Observance Commission, 1966).
19. McRae, *Negroes in Michigan.*
20. John Chavis, *Then Freedom Came...: Detroit and the Emancipation Proclamation* (Detroit Historical Society, 1963).
21. *Detroit Free Press,* January 3, 1863.
22. *Detroit Advertiser & Tribune,* January 3, 1863.

Chapter 3

23. *Detroit Free Press*, March 7, 1863.
24. *Detroit Free Press*, March 7, 1863.
25. *Detroit Free Press*, March 7, 1863.
26. "A Riot in Detroit," in Milton Meltzer's *In Their Own Words: A History of the American Negro, 1619–1865* (Thomas Y. Crowell Company, 1967).
27. Burton Historical Collection, *Negroes in Detroit* (Detroit Public Library).
28. *Detroit Advertiser & Tribune*, March 21, 1863.

Chapter 4

29. *Detroit Advertiser & Tribune*, April 2 and 4, 1864.
30. *Detroit Advertiser & Tribune*, April 14, 1864.

31. *Detroit Free Press*, May 8, 1863; *Detroit Advertiser & Tribune*, April 16 and 22, 1863.

Chapter 5

32. State of Michigan, *Manual Containing the Rules of the Senate and House of Representatives of the State of Michigan* (Hosmer & Kerr, 1861), 93; State of Michigan, *Acts of the Legislature of the State of Michigan Passed at the Extra Session of 1862* (John A. Kerr & Company, 1862), 20–48; *Early History of Michigan with Biographies of State Officers, Members of Congress, Judges and Legislators*, "Henry Barnes" (Thorpe and Godfrey, 1888), 70.
33. McRae, *Negroes in Michigan*; State of Michigan, *Documents Accompanying the Journal of the House of Representatives of the State of Michigan at the Annual Session of 1846*, Document No. 12 (Bagg & Harmon, 1846), 1–4.
34. John Robertson, *Michigan in the War* (W.S. George and Company State Printers and Binders, 1882), 488.
35. Robertson, *Michigan in the War*, 488.
36. Robertson, *Michigan in the War*, 488.
37. Robertson, *Michigan in the War*, 488.
38. Robertson, *Michigan in the War*, 488.
39. Robertson, *Michigan in the War*, 488–89.
40. *Detroit Free Press*, August 21, 1863.
41. *Detroit Free Press*, August 21, 1863.
42. Robertson, *Michigan in the War*, 489.

Chapter 6

43. *Cass Country Republican*, October 8, 1863.
44. Freedmen's Progress Commission, *Michigan Manual of Freedmen's Progress*, comps. Francis H. Warren and John M. Green (1915).
45. Freedmen's Progress Commission, *Michigan Manual of Freedmen's Progress*.
46. *Detroit Advertiser & Tribune*, September 25, 1863.
47. *Detroit Advertiser & Tribune*, September 18, 1863.
48. *Detroit Advertiser & Tribune*, September 18, 1863.
49. *Detroit Advertiser & Tribune*, September 18, 1863.
50. *Detroit Advertiser & Tribune*, September 18, 1863.
51. *Detroit Advertiser & Tribune*, September 29, 1863.

52. *Detroit Advertiser & Tribune*, October 12, 1863.
53. *Detroit Free Press*, October 2, 1863.
54. *Detroit Advertiser & Tribune*, October 14, 1863.
55. *Detroit Advertiser & Tribune*, October 26, 1863.
56. *Detroit Advertiser & Tribune*, October 27, 1863.
57. *Detroit Advertiser & Tribune*, October 30, 1863.
58. *Detroit Advertiser & Tribune*, November 2, 1863.
59. Dr. Curtis, November 12, 1863, in *"This Is a War for the Utter Extinction of Slavery": The Civil War Letters of James Benjamin Franklin Curtis, Hospital Steward, 1st Michigan Colored Infantry*, ed. Robert Beasecker (University Library, Grand Valley State University, 2020).
60. Dr. Curtis, February 19, 1864, in *"This Is a War."*
61. Dr. Curtis, February 19, 1864, in *"This Is a War."*
62. *Detroit Advertiser & Tribune*, November 23, 1863.
63. *Detroit Advertiser & Tribune*, November 23, 1863.
64. Sojourner Truth, *Narrative of Sojourner Truth: A Bondswoman of Olden Times, Emancipated by the New York Legislature in the Early Part of the Present Century with a History of Her Labors and Correspondence* (self-published, 1881), 126.
65. *Evansville Daily*, November 23, 1863; *Detroit Advertiser & Tribune*, November 26, 1863.

Chapter 7

66. *Detroit Free Press*, December 3, 1863.
67. *Detroit Advertiser & Tribune*, December 26, 1863.
68. James M. McPherson, *For Cause and Comrades: Why Men Fought in the Civil War* (Oxford University Press, 2008).
69. E.J. Hess, *The Union Soldier in Battle: Enduring the Ordeal of Combat* (University Press of Kansas, 2009).
70. G.J.W. Urwin, *The United States Infantry: An Illustrated History, 1775–1918* (Sterling Publishing, 1983).
71. *Detroit Advertiser & Tribune*, December 26, 1863.
72. Michael W. Nagle, *The Forgotten Iron King of the Great Lakes: Eber Brock Ward, 1811–1875* (Wayne State University Law Press, 2022)
73. *Detroit Advertiser & Tribune*, November 9, 1863.
74. *Detroit Advertiser & Tribune*, November 9, 1863.
75. *Detroit Advertiser & Tribune*, November 9, 1863.
76. *Detroit Advertiser & Tribune*, November 9, 1863.

Chapter 8

77. *Detroit Advertiser & Tribune*, December 3, 1863.
78. *Detroit Advertiser & Tribune*, December 9, 1863.
79. *Detroit Advertiser & Tribune*, December 9, 1863.
80. *Detroit Advertiser & Tribune*, December 9, 1863.
81. *Detroit Advertiser & Tribune*, December 9, 1863.
82. *Detroit Advertiser & Tribune*, December 9, 1863.
83. *Detroit Advertiser & Tribune*, December 10, 1863.
84. *Detroit Advertiser & Tribune*, December 10, 1863.
85. DeLand Family Papers, 1842–1913, 1816–1984, "History of Jackson County," 166–84; "Mass Convention," *American Citizen*, June 28, 1854; "Mass Convention," *American Citizen*, July 5, 1854.
86. DeLand Family Papers, 1842–1913, 1816–1984, "History of Jackson County," 166–84; "Mass Convention," *American Citizen*, June 28, 1854; "Mass Convention," *American Citizen*, July 5, 1854.
87. DeLand Family Papers, 1842–1913, 1816–1984, "History of Jackson County," 166–84; "Mass Convention," *American Citizen*, June 28, 1854; "Mass Convention," *American Citizen*, July 5, 1854.
88. *Detroit Advertiser & Tribune*, December 10, 1863.
89. *Detroit Advertiser & Tribune*, December 10, 1863.
90. *Detroit Advertiser & Tribune*, December 11, 1863.
91. *Detroit Advertiser & Tribune*, December 11, 1863.
92. *Detroit Advertiser & Tribune*, December 11, 1863.
93. *Detroit Advertiser & Tribune*, December 12, 1863.
94. *Detroit Advertiser & Tribune*, December 12, 1863.
95. *Detroit Advertiser & Tribune*, December 15, 1863.
96. *Detroit Advertiser & Tribune*, December 15, 1863.
97. *Detroit Advertiser & Tribune*, December 15, 1863.
98. William E. Washington, record, 102nd U.S. Colored Troops, National Archives and Records Administration.
99. *Cass County Republican*, December 17, 1863.
100. *Detroit Advertiser & Tribune*, December 11, 1863.
101. Diana Dretske, "Private Henry McIntosh, 102nd U.S. Colored Troops," *Dunn Museum of Lake County*, February 24, 2021.
102. Dretske, "Private Henry McIntosh."
103. Dretske, "Private Henry McIntosh"; *Michigan, Adjutant General's Department, Record of Service of Michigan Volunteers in the Civil War, 1861–1865*, vol. 46 (Ihling Bros. and Everard).

104. Dretske, "Private Henry McIntosh"; *Michigan, Adjutant General's Department, Record of Service of Michigan Volunteers in the Civil War, 1861–1865*, vol. 46 (Ihling Bros. and Everard).
105. Dretske, "Private Henry McIntosh"; *Michigan, Adjutant General's Department, Record of Service of Michigan Volunteers in the Civil War, 1861–1865*, vol. 46 (Ihling Bros. and Everard).

Chapter 9

106. *Detroit Advertiser & Tribune*, December 18, 1863.
107. "Journal of the Prosecution of the War," quoted in McRae, *Negroes in Michigan*, 58.
108. *Detroit Advertiser & Tribune*, December 18 and 19, 1863.
109. *Detroit Advertiser & Tribune*, December 24, 1863.
110. *Detroit Free Press*, December 28, 1863.
111. *Detroit Free Press*, December 28, 1863.
112. *Detroit Free Press*, December 28, 1863.
113. *Detroit Advertiser & Tribune*, January 2, 1864.
114. *Detroit Advertiser & Tribune*, January 4, 1864.
115. *Detroit Advertiser & Tribune*, January 4, 1864.
116. *Detroit Advertiser & Tribune*, January 4, 1864.
117. *Detroit Advertiser & Tribune*, January 13, 1863, quoted in McRae, *Negroes in Michigan*, 59.
118. Michael O. Smith, "Raising a Black Regiment in Michigan: Adversity and Triumph," *Michigan Historical Review* 16, no. 2 (Fall 1990): 28.

Chapter 10

119. *Detroit Advertiser & Tribune*, January 6, 1864.
120. *Detroit Advertiser & Tribune*, January 6, 1864.
121. *Detroit Advertiser & Tribune*, January 6, 1864.
122. *Detroit Advertiser & Tribune*, January 6, 1864.
123. *Detroit Advertiser & Tribune*, January 6, 1864.
124. *Detroit Advertiser & Tribune*, January 6, 1864.
125. "Flag for the Colored Regiment," *Detroit Advertiser & Tribune*, circa late 1863.

Chapter 11

126. *Detroit Free Press*, December 4, 1863.
127. *Detroit Advertiser & Tribune*, February 12, 1864.
128. *Detroit Advertiser & Tribune*, February 12, 1864.
129. *Detroit Advertiser & Tribune*, February 12, 1864.
130. *Detroit Free Press*, February 12, 1864.

Chapter 12

131. *Detroit Tribune*, March 22, 1914.
132. *Detroit Tribune*, March 22, 1914.
133. Richard M. Reid, *African Canadians in Union Blue: Volunteering for the Cause in the Civil War* (University of British Columbia Press, 2014).
134. Reid, *African Canadians in Union Blue.*

Chapter 13

135. McRae, *Negroes in Michigan.*
136. *Detroit Advertiser & Tribune*, February 21, 1864.
137. *Detroit Advertiser & Tribune*, February 21, 1864.
138. John Thompson, record, 102nd U.S. Colored Troops, National Archives and Records Administration; *Detroit Advertiser & Tribune*, February 21, 1864.
139. John Thompson, record, 102nd U.S. Colored Troops, National Archives and Records Administration; *Detroit Advertiser & Tribune*, February 21, 1864.
140. *Detroit Free Press*, February 28, 1864.
141. *Detroit Free Press*, February 28, 1864.
142. *Detroit Advertiser & Tribune*, February 21, 1864.
143. *Detroit Free Press*, March 25, 1864.
144. Dr. Curtis, March 24, 1864, in *"This Is a War."*
145. *Detroit Free Press*, March 25, 1864.
146. *Detroit Free Press*, March 25, 1864.
147. *Detroit Free Press*, March 25, 1864.
148. *Detroit Free Press*, March 29, 1864.
149. *Detroit Free Press*, December 24, 1863.

150. *Detroit Free Press*, February 12, 1864.
151. *Detroit Free Press*, February 12, 1864.
152. *Detroit Free Press*, February 18, 1864.
153. *Detroit Advertiser & Tribune*, March 5, 1864.
154. *Detroit Advertiser & Tribune*, March 5, 1864.
155. *Detroit Advertiser & Tribune*, March 5, 1864.
156. Henry Brown, Director, Detroit Historical Museum, May 20, 1966, conversation with the author.

Chapter 14

157. "From Inmates to Infantrymen: The Michigan Boys' Reform School and the American Civil War," Historical Society of Michigan, 2018.
158. "From Inmates to Infantrymen."
159. *Michigan, Adjutant General's Department, Record of Service of Michigan Volunteers*, vol. 46, 190+.
160. "From Inmates to Infantrymen."
161. "From Inmates to Infantrymen."
162. "From Inmates to Infantrymen."

Chapter 15

163. *Detroit Advertiser & Tribune*, March 11, 1864.
164. *Detroit Free Press*, March 12, 1864.
165. *Detroit Advertiser & Tribune*, March 11, 1864.
166. Dr. Curtis, May 11, 1864, in *"This Is a War."*
167. *Detroit Advertiser & Tribune*, March 16, 1864.
168. DeAnne Blanton and Lauren M. Cook, *They Fought Like Demons: Women Soldiers in the American Civil War* (Louisiana State University Press, 2002).
169. *Detroit Advertiser & Tribune*, March 19, 1864.
170. Dr. Curtis, March 24, 1864, in *"This Is a War."*
171. *Detroit Advertiser & Tribune*, March 28, 1864.
172. *Detroit Advertiser & Tribune*, March 28, 1864.

Chapter 16

173. *Detroit Free Press*, March 29, 1864; April 1, 1864.
174. *Detroit Advertiser & Tribune*, March 30, 1864.
175. *Detroit Advertiser & Tribune*, March 30, 1864.
176. *Detroit Advertiser & Tribune*, March 30, 1864.
177. *Detroit Advertiser & Tribune*, October 30, 1863.
178. *Detroit Advertiser & Tribune*, March 30, 1864.
179. *Wilbur Nelson Diary*, 1864, Wilbur Nelson Papers, Collection c.00159, Michigan State University Archives and Historical Collections, East Lansing, Michigan, MSU Libraries Digital Repository; Dr. Curtis, April 4, 1864, in *"This Is a War."*
180. Dr. Curtis, April 4, 1864, in *"This Is a War."*
181. *Detroit Advertiser & Tribune*, April 5, 1864.
182. Dr. Curtis, April 4, 1864, in *"This Is a War"*; Wilbur Nelson Diary, April 1, 1864.
183. Dr. Curtis, April 4, 1864, in *"This Is a War."*
184. Dr. Curtis, April 4, 1864, in *"This Is a War"*; *Detroit Advertiser & Tribune*, April 5, 1864.
185. Dr. Curtis, April 4, 1864, in *"This Is a War"*; *Detroit Advertiser & Tribune*, April 8, 1864.
186. Dr. Curtis, April 4, 1864, in *"This Is a War."*
187. *Detroit Advertiser & Tribune*, April 8, 1864.
188. Henry Barns, record, 102nd U.S. Colored Troops, National Archives and Records Administration.
189. Dr. Curtis, May 1864, in *"This Is a War."*
190. Barns, record, NARA.
191. *Detroit Advertiser & Tribune*, May 31, 1864.
192. Wilbur Nelson Diary, April 23, 1864.
193. Robertson, *Michigan in the War.*
194. Letter from William W. Fish, 11th New Hampshire, April 14, 1864, New Hampshire Historical Society.
195. *American Citizen*, April 27, 1864.
196. Dr. Curtis, April 7, 1864, in *"This Is a War."*
197. Dr. Curtis, April 12, 1864, in *"This Is a War."*
198. Wilbur Nelson Diary, April 13, 1864; *Detroit Advertiser & Tribune*, April 20, 1864.
199. Wilbur Nelson Diary, April 13, 1864; *Detroit Advertiser & Tribune*, April 20, 1864.

200. Wilbur Nelson Diary, April 14, 1864.
201. Dr. Curtis, April 18, 1864, in *"This Is a War."*
202. Private Murray, May 2, 1864, in *Private No More: The Civil War Letters of John Lovejoy Murray, 102nd United States Colored Infantry*, ed. Sharon A. Roger Hepburn (University of Georgia Press, 2023).
203. Dr. Curtis, April 18, 1864, in *"This Is a War."*
204. Wilbur Nelson Diary, April 19, 1864.
205. Wilbur Nelson Diary, April 27, 1864.
206. "Black Soldiers in the U.S. Military During the Civil War," National Archives, https://www.archives.gov.
207. Dr. Curtis, May 12, 1864, in *"This Is a War."*
208. *Detroit Advertiser & Tribune*, June 7, 1864.
209. Dr. Curtis, May 1, 1864, in *"This Is a War."*
210. Dr. Curtis, May 16, 1864, in *"This Is a War."*
211. Private Murray, July 3, 1864, in *Private No More.*
212. Dr. Curtis, May 1, 1864, in *"This Is a War."*
213. Robertson, *Michigan in the War.*
214. Private Murray, May 2, 1864, in *Private No More.*
215. *Detroit Advertiser & Tribune*, May 23, 1864.
216. Private Murray, May 19, 1864, in *Private No More.*
217. *Detroit Advertiser & Tribune*, June 7, 1864.
218. Private Murray, May 19, 1864, in *Private No More.*
219. Wilbur Nelson Diary, May 17, 1864.
220. Dr. Curtis, May 12, 1864, in *"This Is a War."*
221. "Fort Monroe and the 'Contrabands of War,'" National Park Service.
222. James Oliver Horton and Lois E. Horton, *Slavery and the Making of America* (Oxford University Press, 2005); Drew Gilpin Faust, *This Republic of Suffering: Death and the American Civil War* (Alfred A. Knopf, 2008).
223. McPherson, *Battle Cry of Freedom*; Patricia C. McKissack and Fredrick McKissack, *Sojourner Truth: Ain't I a Woman?* (Scholastic, 1993).
224. William Waring, record, 102nd U.S. Colored Troops, National Archives and Records Administration.
225. Obituary from *Howard University Journal*, published in 1900, Washington, D.C.
226. Dr. Curtis, May 16, 1864, in *"This Is a War."*
227. Dr. Curtis, May 16, 1864, in *"This Is a War."*
228. *Detroit Advertiser & Tribune*, June 7, 1864.
229. Hess, *Union Soldier in Battle.*
230. McPherson, *For Cause and Comrades.*

231. Private Murray, June 13, 1864, in *Private No More.*
232. U.S. War Department, "General Order 143," May 22, 1863, Washington, D.C., 1863, available via National Archives and Records Administration.
233. National Archives and Records Administration, "Black Soldiers in the Civil War," National Archives Educator Resources, March 19, 2019.
234. *Detroit Advertiser & Tribune,* June 21, 1864.
235. Private Murray, June 13, 1864, in *Private No More.*
236. McPherson, *For Cause and Comrades.*
237. Dr. Curtis, June 18, 1864, in *"This Is a War."*
238. Dr. Curtis, June 21, 1864, in *"This Is a War."*
239. *Detroit Advertiser & Tribune,* June 21, 1864.
240. Charlotte Forten, *The Journal of Charlotte Forten: A Free Black Girl Before the Civil War,* ed. Brenda Stevenson (originally printed in 1864; reprinted by Houghton Mifflin, 1981).
241. American Missionary Association, annual report, 1865, Internet Archive.

Chapter 17

242. Wilbur Nelson Diary, June 23, 1864.
243. Dr. Curtis, June 21, 1864, in *"This Is a War."*
244. Wilbur Nelson Diary, June 1864.
245. *Detroit Advertiser & Tribune,* July 18, 2024.
246. *Detroit Advertiser & Tribune,* July 18, 2024.
247. *Small Arms Used by Michigan Troops in the Civil War* (Michigan Civil War Centennial Observance Commission, 1966).
248. Dr. Curtis, July 5, 1864, in *"This Is a War."*
249. Dr. Curtis, July 5, 1864, in *"This Is a War."*
250. Wilbur Nelson Diary, July 7 1864.
251. Dr. Curtis, August 5, 1864, in *"This Is a War."*
252. Private Murray, July 10, 1864, in *Private No More.*
253. Dr. Curtis, July 1864, in *"This Is a War."*
254. Dr. Curtis, July 1864, in *"This Is a War."*
255. David W. Blight, *Race and Reunion: The Civil War in American Memory* (Harvard University Press, 2001); Horton and Horton, *In Hope of Liberty.*
256. Blight, *Race and Reunion*; Horton and Horton, *In Hope of Liberty.*
257. Blight, *Race and Reunion*; Horton and Horton, *In Hope of Liberty.*

258. Blight, *Race and Reunion*; Horton and Horton, *In Hope of Liberty*.
259. Wilbur Nelson Diary, August 1864; William E. Sleight, *Lieutenant William E. Sleight Memoir*, March 16, 1917, Michigan State University Archives & Historical Collections, Manuscript.
260. Private Murray, August 14, 1864, in *Private No More*.
261. Wilbur Nelson Diary, August 1864; Sleight, *Lieutenant William E. Sleight Memoir*; Robertson, *Michigan in the War*.
262. Wilbur Nelson Diary, August 1864; Sleight, *Lieutenant William E. Sleight Memoir*; Robertson, *Michigan in the War*.
263. Wilbur Nelson Diary, August 1864.
264. Wilbur Nelson Diary, August 19, 1864.
265. Alonzo Reed, letter to his mother, September 2, 1864, *Alonzo Reed Letters*, 1864–66, David M. Rubenstein Rare Book & Manuscript Library, Duke University.
266. Private Murray, August 20, 1864, in *Private No More*.
267. National Archives and Records Administration, Courts-Martial Records, Washington, D.C.
268. Robertson, *Michigan in the War*.
269. Wilbur Nelson Diary, October 16, 1864.
270. Wilbur Nelson, *Wilbur Nelson Papers*, November 24, 1864, Michigan State University Archives & Historical Collections.
271. Wilbur Nelson Diary; Dr. Curtis, in *"This Is a War."*
272. Private Murray, date unknown, in *Private No More*; Dr. Curtis, in *"This Is a War."*
273. Wilbur Nelson Diary, November 29, 1864.
274. Bert Dunkerly, "The War in the Lowcountry, Part II: The Battle of Honey Hill," *Emerging Civil War*, November 30, 2023.
275. Dunkerly, "War in the Lowcountry, Part II."
276. *Detroit Advertiser & Tribune*, October 17, 1865; Murray, *Private No More*.
277. Walter F. Beyer and Oscar F. Keydel, *Deeds of Valor: How America's Heroes Won the Medal of Honor* (Perrien-Keydel Company, 1902).
278. *Detroit Advertiser & Tribune*, December 20, 1864.
279. Robertson, *Michigan in the War*.
280. Robertson, *Michigan in the War*; *Detroit Advertiser & Tribune*, December 22, 1864; Luis F. Emilio, *A Brave Black Regiment: History of the Fifty-Fourth Regiment of Massachusetts Volunteer Infantry, 1863–1865* (Boston Book Company, 1891).

Chapter 18

281. Edwin S. Redkey, *A Grand Army of Black Men: Letters from African-American Soldiers in the Union Army, 1861–1865* (Cambridge University Press, 1993).
282. Redkey, *Grand Army of Black Men.*
283. Redkey, *Grand Army of Black Men.*
284. Robertson, *Michigan in the War*; Wilbur Nelson Diary, February 1865.
285. Wilbur Nelson Diary, February 1865; Sleight, *Lieutenant William E. Sleight Memoir.*
286. Sleight, *Lieutenant William E. Sleight Memoir*; *Detroit Advertiser & Tribune*, May 31, 1865.
287. Wilbur Nelson Diary, February 1865.
288. Dr. Curtis, March 14, 1865, in *"This Is a War."*
289. Dr. Curtis, March 19, 1865, in *"This Is a War."*
290. Dr. Curtis, March 19, 1865, in *"This Is a War."*
291. Wilbur Nelson Diary, March 28, 1865; Robertson, *Michigan in the War.*
292. Dr. Curtis, April 2, 1865, in *"This Is a War."*

Chapter 19

293. Sleight, *Lieutenant William E. Sleight Memoir.*
294. Sleight, *Lieutenant William E. Sleight Memoir.*
295. Sleight, *Lieutenant William E. Sleight Memoir.*
296. Sleight, *Lieutenant William E. Sleight Memoir.*
297. Sleight, *Lieutenant William E. Sleight Memoir.*
298. Sleight, *Lieutenant William E. Sleight Memoir.*
299. Sleight, *Lieutenant William E. Sleight Memoir.*
300. Sleight, *Lieutenant William E. Sleight Memoir.*
301. Sleight, *Lieutenant William E. Sleight Memoir*; Congressional Medal of Honor Society.
302. Sleight, *Lieutenant William E. Sleight Memoir*; Congressional Medal of Honor Society; Robertson, *Michigan in the War.*

Chapter 20

303. Emilio, *Brave Black Regiment*; *Detroit Advertiser & Tribune*, May 31, 1865.

304. Emilio, *Brave Black Regiment*; *Detroit Advertiser & Tribune*, May 31, 1865.
305. Emilio, *Brave Black Regiment*; *Detroit Advertiser & Tribune*, May 31, 1865.
306. Emilio, *Brave Black Regiment*; *Detroit Advertiser & Tribune*, May 31, 1865.
307. Emilio, *Brave Black Regiment*; *Detroit Advertiser & Tribune*, May 31, 1865.
308. Emilio, *Brave Black Regiment*; *Detroit Advertiser & Tribune*, May 31, 1865.
309. Emilio, *Brave Black Regiment*; *Detroit Advertiser & Tribune*, May 31, 1865.
310. Emilio, *Brave Black Regiment*; *Detroit Advertiser & Tribune*, May 31, 1865.
311. Emilio, *Brave Black Regiment*; *Detroit Advertiser & Tribune*, May 31, 1865.

Chapter 21

312. Sleight, *Lieutenant William E. Sleight Memoir.*
313. Sleight, *Lieutenant William E. Sleight Memoir.*
314. Emilio, *Brave Black Regiment.*
315. Emilio, *Brave Black Regiment.*
316. Robertson, *Michigan in the War.*
317. Sleight, *Lieutenant William E. Sleight Memoir*; Wilbur Nelson Letters, 1865.
318. Dr. Curtis, July 13, 1865, in *"This Is a War."*
319. Sleight, *Lieutenant William E. Sleight Memoir*; Dr. Curtis, June 17, 1866, in *"This Is a War."*
320. Sleight, *Lieutenant William E. Sleight Memoir.*
321. Dr. Curtis, July 17, 1865, in *"This Is a War."*
322. Dr. Curtis, May 13, 1865, in *"This Is a War."*
323. Dr. Curtis, May 38, 1865, in *"This Is a War."*
324. Dr. Curtis, May 38, 1865, in *"This Is a War."*
325. Wilbur Nelson Diary, September & October 1865; Robertson, *Michigan in the War.*
326. Wilbur Nelson Diary, October 1865.
327. *Detroit Free Press*, October 20, 1865.
328. Wilbur Nelson Diary, October 1865.
329. Sleight, *Lieutenant William E. Sleight Memoir.*

Chapter 23

330. Henry Chipman, "Report of Col. Henry L. Chipman, One Hundred and Second U.S. Colored Troops, of Operations April 11–25," in *The War of the Rebellion: A Compilation of the Official Records of the Union and*

Confederate Armies, Series 1, Vol. 47, No. 278 (Government Printing Office, 1895), 1,039–40.

331. Michigan State Capitol, Save the Flags organization, 2021.
332. Michigan State Capitol, Save the Flags organization, 2021.
333. *Lansing State Republican*, August 29, 1866.
334. "The Murderer in Ingham County," *Detroit Free Press*, August 28, 1866; "A Horrible Crime," *Lansing State Republican*, August 29, 1866, 8; "The Lynching of the Delhi Murderer," *Detroit Free Press*, August 31, 1866; "The Delhi Tragedy," *Hillsdale Standard*, September 4, 1866; Jacob McCormick, "Reckoning with a Troubled Past: The John Taylor Lynching," *Chronicle* 44, no. 1 (Spring 2021): 17–18.
335. "The Murderer in Ingham County," *Detroit Free Press*, August 28, 1866; "A Horrible Crime," *Lansing State Republican*, August 29, 1866, 8; "The Lynching of the Delhi Murderer," *Detroit Free Press*, August 31, 1866; "The Delhi Tragedy," *Hillsdale Standard*, September 4, 1866; Jacob McCormick, "Reckoning with a Troubled Past: The John Taylor Lynching," *Chronicle* 44, no. 1 (Spring 2021): 17–18.
336. Keith G. Harrison, *Cass County, Michigan in the Civil War and Grand Army of the Republic* (Michigan's Grand Army of the Republic Memorial Hall and Museum, 2020); Freedmen's Progress Commission, *Michigan Manual of Freedmen's Progress*.
337. Harrison, *Cass County, Michigan in the Civil War*; Freedmen's Progress Commission, *Michigan Manual of Freedmen's Progress*.
338. *Ann Arbor Courier-Register*, August 6, 1884.
339. *Ann Arbor Courier-Register*, August 6, 1884.
340. *Cassopolis Vigilant*, August 6, 1891.
341. Grand Rapids Historical Commission, "Grand Rapids and the Civil War."
342. McRae, *Negroes in Michigan*.

Chapter 24

343. House Resolution 125, 2021, Michigan legislature.
344. Michigan Historical Center, Historical Marker Archives.
345. Michigan Historical Center, Historical Marker Archives.
346. Michigan Historical Center, Historical Marker Archives.
347. John Allen White Jr., *Soldiers of the Cross: The African American Journey from Slavery to the Promised Land* (self-published, 2016).

348. *Times Herald* (Port Huron, MI), February 6, 1998.
349. "Remembering the United States Colored Troops Who Helped Win the Civil War," *USA Today*, May 31, 2021.
350. Michigan Legislature Archive.
351. "I-375 Gets New Name Honoring Detroit Regiment that Fought in Civil War," FOX 2 Detroit, March 29, 2021.

About the Author

Maurice Imhoff is a Michigan historian specializing in the state's African American Civil War regiment, the 1st Michigan Colored Infantry. In 2020, he cofounded the Jackson County Michigan Historical Society, where he actively promotes local history. Maurice's passion for history earned an internship at the Smithsonian National Museum of American History, where he collaborated with curators from the Division of Cultural and Community Life and the Division of Political and Military History. Committed to highlighting marginalized communities, Maurice continues to engage the public through lectures, writing and community projects, ensuring that these vital stories are not forgotten.